Christmas

BAKING

Christmas BAKING

Festive Cookies, Candies,

Cakes, Breads, and Snacks

to Bring Comfort and Joy

to Your Holiday

JOYCE & LAURA KLYNSTRA

GOOD BOOKS, NEW YORK

Good Books books may be purchased in bulk at special discounts for sales promotion, corporate gifts, fund-raising, or educational purposes. Special editions can also be created to specifications. For details, contact the Special Sales Department, Good Books, 307 West 36th Street, 11th Floor, New York, NY 10018 or info@skyhorsepublishing.com.

Good Books is an imprint of Skyhorse Publishing, Inc®, a Delaware corporation.

Visit our website at www.goodbooks.com

10 9 8 7 6 5 4 3 2 1

Library of Congress Cataloging-in-Publication Data is available on file.

Cover and interior design and photography by Laura Klynstra

Print ISBN: 978-1-68099-646-3
eBook ISBN: 978-1-68099-647-0

Printed in China

for my grandkids
joseph, megan, matthew, levi, leo, victor, and johan

who bring me so much joy

—J.K.

for my boys
leo and victor

may all your christmases be sweet

—L.K.

CONTENTS

"If baking is any labor at all, it's a labor of love. A love that gets passed from generation to generation."

—REGINA BRETT

INTRODUCTION

———— • ————

"Christmas is a bridge. We need bridges as the river of time flows past.
Today's Christmas should mean creating happy hours for
tomorrow and reliving those of yesterday."
—GLADYS TABER

Part of the appeal of Christmas is the many memories we bring to the season. Attic boxes filled with tinsel, garland, and delicate glass ornaments come out once a year and remind us of the anticipation and magic of our childhoods. We have songs we only listen to in December and recipes that are especially for this time of the year. The fragrance of cinnamon baking can fill you with an intangible nostalgia that is part memories of baking with a parent or grandparent, part seeing your own child's holiday excitement, and part thinking of how he will remember today in years to come.

I recall sitting on the kitchen counter when I was too small to see over its edge. I watched my mom mix cookie dough, sitting cross-legged by the bowl. The vision of butter, sugar, and eggs coming together and the smell of vanilla is at the root of my love of baking. At Christmastime, my mom rolled out and baked gingerbread people then set my brother and me to decorate them with paintbrushes and colored Wilton candy melts in coffee mugs placed in hot water. Now my son, Leo, loves to climb onto the counter to help make cookies almost as much as he enjoys eating them.

Even before I had a family of my own, I loved baking for the holidays. When I lived in Jersey City, my friend Allison would come for a weekend baking fest. Allison made bars and truffles while I piped designs on sugar cookies with royal icing. At the end, we divided the lot, and we each carried heavy bags on the PATH to our offices in New York to share with our colleagues.

Christmas baking is all about love and sharing—it's filled with tradition and comfort.

My mom and I decided to write this book to celebrate that joy. We have assembled these recipes from years of baking at home for our family and friends. Whether you're baking for colleagues, a church bake sale, a big family, or a small circle of friends, we hope you'll find a few new favorites to incorporate into your traditions. Have fun, make memories, and enjoy a sweet Christmas!

—*Laura*

LAURA'S NOTES ON INGREDIENTS

---•---

High-quality ingredients make high-quality desserts. So always buy the best ingredients you can afford. If you can only splurge on a couple ingredients, make them chocolate and vanilla. There's a huge difference between high-quality chocolate and vanilla and the cheaper versions.

BUTTER

Butter is the base ingredient for most desserts and is vital to baking success. Always use unsalted butter. One can never tell how much salt is in the salted variety, so the only way to control how much salt goes into a recipe is to use unsalted butter. Unsalted butter also works better when browning butter, as salted butter foams more, making it more difficult to see the moment the butter starts to brown.

Butter is best creamed with sugar at room temperature. If you need to bring butter to room temperature quickly, slice it into ½-inch slices and lay it on a plate or parchment for 10 to 15 minutes. If you do use a microwave, be careful not to let the butter melt—runny or melted butter does not work well in most recipes.

DAIRY

Always use full-fat milk and buttermilk in recipes for best results. Buying local dairy brands will get you the freshest dairy while supporting local farmers. Milk from grass-fed cows is the most natural and is my preference when I can afford it.

EGGS

We raise chickens and ducks that roam and forage in our yard and woods from dawn to dusk. Birds that live natural lives as omnivores produce the best, most vitamin-rich eggs that are perfect for baking. Not everyone has the time or inclination to raise their own birds, but eggs from local producers of pasture-raised hens in your neighborhood or at famers' markets are the next best thing. You can also purchase naturally raised eggs in most supermarkets. Look for pasture-raised versus free range or cage free. Avoid eggs that say vegetarian-fed, as the only way to make a hen into a vegetarian is to deny her access to the outdoors. You know you have a good egg when the yolk is much closer to orange than yellow.

Recipes in this book were tested with chicken eggs. If you do happen to have duck eggs, I recommend trying them in cakes. The higher fat content in the yolk of a duck egg gives more rise and flavor to cakes. You can replace one chicken egg with one duck egg as long as it's not too much larger than a chicken egg.

Most recipes in this book call for room-temperature eggs. If you're like me, you never remember to take your eggs out of the refrigerator hours in advance of baking. To bring eggs to room temperature quickly, place in a bowl with warm tap water for about 10 minutes.

FLOUR

Most of the recipes in the book were tested with unbleached all-purpose flour. Many of the cakes use cake flour, which is a finer, more delicate flour that rises better and produces a finer crumb. If you don't have cake flour in the house, you can replace cake flour with all-purpose flour. Your cake might not be quite as lofty, but it will still be delicious.

BAKING SODA AND BAKING POWDER

These ingredients don't age well and can get clumpy with time. They aren't super expensive, so replace often for best results.

SUGAR

Sugar is an important part of most baked recipes, so be sure to keep granulated, light and dark brown sugar, and confectioners' sugar on hand over the holidays. Coarse sugar in a variety of colors will also come in handy when baking for Christmas.

MOLASSES

Always select unsulfured molasses. Cheaper varieties use sulfur dioxide to preserve immature sugarcane and can alter the flavor. Unsulfured molasses is produced from mature sugarcane that doesn't require preservatives and has a richer, sweeter flavor.

MAPLE SYRUP

The most essential thing to remember with maple syrup is to only use the real stuff. Look for *pure* on the label. Inexpensive syrups are usually corn syrup with artificial flavors and should never be used in recipes that call for maple syrup. The real thing is pricey, but it's worth it. Select grade B for a darker syrup with richer flavor.

COCOA POWDER

There are two readily available forms of cocoa powder: unsweetened cocoa powder and Dutch process cocoa powder. Unsweetened or natural cocoa powder is the one most of us grew up using from the Hershey's can. If a recipe doesn't specify which cocoa powder to use, this would be the go-to. Natural cocoa powder is acidic and bitter. Dutch process removes some of the acidity and produces a mellow flavor. Since baking soda requires acidity to raise baked goods, natural cocoa powder is the best choice when paired with baking soda. The two powders are not interchangeable in baked recipes. You can, however, swap them in frostings or hot chocolate. Flavors will also vary based on brand.

VANILLA

Vanilla is the heart of flavor in baking—the most essential extract to keep in your pantry. Pure vanilla extract is made from dried vanilla beans soaked in alcohol for months—not to be confused with imitation vanilla, which is chemically synthesized vanillin flavor—only one of vanilla's three hundred flavors. Real vanilla is complex and adds depth to every recipe. It is the second most expensive spice (after saffron) in the world. In this book, we use three kinds of vanilla: extract, bean paste, and beans. Vanilla bean paste and beans have stronger flavor and will also add dark, tiny flecks to your baked good. Buying vanilla beans individually is very pricey. Buying in bulk is the best way to go. If you don't bake enough to do that, use bean paste in place of vanilla beans to save money.

OTHER EXTRACTS

We use almond extract, maple extract, peppermint extract, and rose water in this book. The main thing to look for when shopping for extracts is *pure* on the label. Try to avoid artificial flavors.

NUTS AND NUT BUTTERS

I once destroyed a pan of Magic Bars by using pecans that had gone bad. Always check your nuts for freshness before adding them to your recipe. Purchase the freshest nuts you can find, and store them in an airtight container after opening.

Peanut butter recipes in this book were all tested with smooth peanut butter like Jif or Skippy. Though I appreciate natural nut butters, I've found the smooth peanut butter to be easier to work with while baking.

Dutch Process Cocoa

Unsweetened Cocoa

WORKING WITH CHOCOLATE

Chocolate is divine but can also be a nightmare. I've had my fair share of chocolate failures—microwaving just a tad too long resulting in scorched chocolate or a little water getting in the pan and the whole batch seizing. Here are a few tips to help the process go smoothly.

CHOCOLATE CHIPS

Chocolate chips are intended to hold their form in chocolate chip cookies and are not ideal for melting, especially for chocolate-dipped confections. Best practice is to use chocolate sold in bar form for melting. You can melt chocolate chips for use in batters, doughs, and party mixes. The quality of the brand will impact how well they melt. I recommend Ghirardelli and Guittard chips both for flavor and workability.

CHOCOLATE FEVES AND WAFERS

Unlike chocolate chips, these chocolate disks are meant to be melted, and they make working with chocolate much easier. Valrhona makes feves that taste amazing and melt into an easy-to-work-with consistency. Their price and limited availability make using them a little impractical. You can purchase them directly on Valrhona's website or through Amazon. Guittard's chocolate wafers are a little more affordable, but they're still difficult to find in stores. You can order them directly from Guittard or through King Arthur Flour. See Resources (page 253) for more information.

CHOCOLATE BARS

Chocolate bars are probably the most practical and easy to come by. Check in the baking aisle for baking bars. Select the percentage of cacao that you like best. Many of the recipes in this book call for bittersweet chocolate with 60 to 70 percent cacao. Since there's usually a lot of sugar elsewhere in a recipe, I find that a dark chocolate gives confections balance and richness. If you prefer semisweet or even milk chocolate, change up the recipe to your favorite. For best flavor, look for premium chocolate brands.

CANDY MELTS

Technically not chocolate, candy melts can be used instead of chocolate to make life easier. Wilton makes a wide array of candy melts you can find in craft stores. Ghirardelli now has a version in most grocery stores called chocolate-flavored melting wafers. Be sure to read the label when shopping for chocolate so you know what you're getting. Working with candy melts is easier, but they don't taste as good as the real thing.

MELTING CHOCOLATE

When melting chocolate, water is your enemy. Make sure your bowl or pot is completely dry before adding your chocolate. Water, even a small amount, can make chocolate seize.

You can melt chocolate in a heatproof bowl in the microwave. Set microwave at 50 percent power and start with 30 seconds. Check chocolate and stir. Continue microwaving in 15-second intervals until almost completely melted. At this point, you can continue to stir until completely melted. I like this method for chocolate that goes in batters and doughs.

Alternately, use a double boiler to melt chocolate. If you don't have a set of pans specifically designed to be a double boiler, you can use a heatproof bowl over a saucepan. Fill the bottom pan with water; the water should not touch the top pan or bowl. Heat water over medium-low heat. Don't bring the water to a boil. Chocolate should be melted slowly. When chocolate is three quarters melted, turn off heat and stir with a rubber spatula until completely melted. Remove the top pan and dry any condensation from the bottom with a towel. Chocolate should now be ready to coat confections. If chocolate starts to cool and become too thick to work with, return it to bottom pan, with stove set to medium low, just until chocolate is smooth again.

THINNING CHOCOLATE

Sometimes melted chocolate isn't thin enough for easy coating. Chocolate that is too thick might come out clumpy or too thick on your finished candy. Mixing in vegetable shortening or oil will help thin chocolate. Start with 1 teaspoon. You should use the least amount necessary. Never add butter, as butter always has a small percentage of water content and could result in your chocolate seizing. Paramount crystals are another great way to thin chocolate. Add ½ teaspoon at a time until you reach a workable consistency.

TEMPERING CHOCOLATE

Chocolate that is in temper will appear smooth and shiny and will snap when broken. Untempered chocolate may be dull, clumpy, and have white streaks. Not everyone has the time or patience for what basically amounts to an exercise in chemistry—to align cocoa butter crystals within the chocolate through temperature changes and stirring. If you don't want to mess with tempering, follow best practices for melting chocolate. Be careful not to overheat and your confections will still taste great.

If you're aiming for a shiny, smooth appearance on your chocolate-covered goodies, follow these steps.

1. Finely chop chocolate. Melt two thirds of chocolate with either a double boiler or microwave. Be careful not to overheat chocolate. Use an instant-read thermometer to check temperature while melting chocolate. Follow the chart below and do not exceed the high temperature listed.

2. After chocolate is melted, remove from heat and add remaining chocolate in 3 to 4 additions. Stir constantly until each addition has melted. Continue to stir and monitor temperature until it cools to the in-temper temperature on the chart below. This can take some patience, but it is important to keep stirring, as the agitation will help achieve the proper crystallization.

3. Once the chocolate has cooled to the desired temperature, it will need to be reheated slightly to a working temperature. It will not take much heat to raise the temperature, so watch carefully and do not use excessive heat. Raising the temperature above the working temperature listed in the chart may put chocolate out of temper and require starting over.

4. Work efficiently to dip chocolate. Stop periodically to stir chocolate and heat it back to working temperature if it cools too much while working.

	DARK CHOCOLATE	MILK CHOCOLATE	WHITE CHOCOLATE
Do not exceed temperature while melting	135°F	122°F	115°F
Cool to temperature for chocolate to be in temper	84°F	81°F	79°F
Reheat to workable temperature	88–90°F	86–88°F	82–84°F

TIPS

* Work with a high-quality chocolate for best results and avoid chocolate chips.

* Tempering works best with a room temperature between 60 and 68°F. High humidity and high room temperatures may make tempering fail even if you follow all the other steps.

* Work with a pound of chocolate or more for best results. Pour unused chocolate onto parchment and allow to set. Store in an airtight container to use at later time. Chocolate will keep for up to a year.

NOTES ON EQUIPMENT

STAND OR HAND MIXER

A stand mixer is the most valuable tool to the home baker. It's perfect for bread dough and whipping cream or egg whites. It's also very convenient for a simple batch of cookies. If you do a lot of baking, a high-quality stand mixer is worth the investment. They are not infallible, however; my KitchenAid mixer has a small pocket at the bottom of the metal bowl that leaves ingredients unmixed. It's very important while using a stand mixer to stop and scrape the sides and bottom of the bowl to ensure even mixing.

If you only have a hand mixer, you can still make most of the recipes in this book with ease. I love a hand mixer for doubling recipes that won't fit in my stand mixer's bowl. You just have to put in a little more effort into mixing with a hand mixer—especially for the time-intensive mixing for meringue or shortbread.

KITCHEN SCALE

The best method for measuring ingredients is a kitchen scale, but like many home cooks, I use measuring cups and spoons for most of my ingredients. A kitchen scale can be nice when measuring chocolate. I also love using a scale for measuring sticky ingredients like peanut butter. You'll find weight equivalencies listed for peanut butter and chocolate throughout this book.

FINE MESH SIEVE

This tool comes in handy when working with cocoa powder, which is almost always clumpy. Even a tiny clump can make a mess of a recipe. Always run cocoa through a sieve or sifter before using. Sieves are also nice for dusting confectioners' sugar.

BAKING SHEETS AND NONSTICK MATS

My favorite way to bake cookies for even results is in a heavy jelly roll pan with a silicone baking mat such as Silpat. I baked without the mats for years, and they aren't essential, but they do make life easier and are worth the investment if you do a lot of baking.

ROLLING PINS AND PASTRY BOARDS

There are many rolling pin options out there. I've used many kinds, but my go-to is a simple wood rolling pin from Williams Sonoma. If you have natural stone countertops, you already have the perfect surface to roll out dough. If you don't, a marble pastry board is great for rolling out piecrusts and cookies. Marble is naturally cooler than other surfaces and helps keep butter cool while working with dough.

DOUBLE BOILER

This is an essential tool for melting chocolate. Melting chocolate for a batter or dough works fine in the microwave, but a double boiler is important when coating confections. If you don't have one, a metal bowl over a medium saucepan will also work.

THERMOMETERS

Ovens can be off from what you expect. Oven thermometers are inexpensive and can help ensure you are baking at the right temperature. A clip-on candy thermometer is essential for making some recipes like toffee, brittles, and fudge.

MEASURING CUPS AND SPOONS

Always use liquid measuring cups for liquids and dry measuring cups for dry ingredients. When measuring powder ingredients like flour or confectioners' sugar, first fluff it by stirring a bit. Then scoop to overfill measuring cup. With the flat edge of a butter knife, scrape off excess. Never pack in flour or confectioners' sugar.

COOKIE SCOOPS

Cookie scoops are essential if you make cookies often. They portion dough and mold it into the perfect shape all while making scooping easier. They come in a variety of sizes. The 4-teaspoon scoop is perfect for drop cookies and the 2-teaspoon size is perfect for truffles and other confections. You can find them at baking supply stores like King Arthur Flour.

COOKIE CUTTERS AND STAMPS

A collection of shaped cookie cutters is essential for creative cookie baking. It is also nice to have a simple set of various-sized round cookie cutters for simple cookie rounds and doughnuts. Linzer cookie cutters are handy for sandwich cookies. Cookie stamps are now commonly available at craft stores. They make a simple shortbread cookie pretty with ease. For suggestions on finding cookie cutters and stamps, see Resources on page 253.

PASTRY BAGS AND TIPS

I like to keep both reusable and disposable pastry bags on hand. The 12-inch disposable bags are nice when making many colors, as cleanup is easier. The 16-inch or larger reusable bags work great for meringue-based cookies like macarons. For piping royal icing on cookies, I prefer a #3 round tip. Large open star or #12 round or larger tips are great for meringue cookies.

BAKING TIPS

* Read the recipe all the way through before starting. That way you'll know if you have all the ingredients, equipment, and time needed for a given recipe.

* Temperature matters when mixing ingredients. The emulsification of fats and liquid is best achieved when ingredients are close to the same temperature. If you have your butter and sugar nicely creamed and fluffy and then add cold eggs, you can get unwanted clumping of butter.

* Throughout this book, you will notice baking time ranges rather than one set time. All ovens are different, and you would be surprised how far off some are from their set temperature. It's always wise to check cookies for visual cues of doneness. Cakes can be tested by inserting a cake tester or toothpick into the top of a cake. Your cake is ready when the knife comes out clean.

* Most recipes will call for mixing the dry ingredients separately from the liquid ingredients. Don't skip this step, as it helps ensure even distribution of salt and leaveners. This is important for even baking, but it also ensures no one gets a bite of cookie that tastes like baking soda.

* For best results, place your oven rack in the center of your oven and bake only one sheet of cookies at a time.

* When baking cakes, never fill your pan more than three quarters full. Sometimes you may not have the same size pan a recipe calls for. You can still make the recipe, just don't overfill your pan. A cake baking over in your oven is a mess and a real hassle to clean up. If your pan is smaller than needed for a given recipe, just bake extra batter in a muffin tin or ramekin. Think of it as a bonus mini cake for the baker.

* It's rare that a batch of fresh cookies or scones gets eaten right out of the oven. Homemade baked goods all taste best on the day they were baked, so if you know you won't eat them all immediately, package a portion and freeze them as soon as they have cooled. The sooner you freeze them, the closer they will be to their original fresh state when you thaw them out. I recommend thawing baked goods in a 290°F oven just until they are warm throughout, usually about 12 to 15 minutes for a muffin or similarly sized baked good.

* Many Christmas recipes are special; it's fun to slow down and work alongside family to add extra flair and decoration. However, there are many times over the holidays when we don't have any extra time to make complicated recipes. We've marked fast and easy recipes in this book with this stamp so you can easily find recipes to make when you're short on time.

RECIPES

CHAPTER

1

THERE'S NO TREAT AS ESSENTIAL

to Christmas as cookies. Kids love to leave a plate for Santa and sneak one for
themselves. Neighbors and friends gather to swap their favorites. It's a joy to see a
box or tray with a colorful variety of classics and new flavors. This chapter covers
many old-fashioned Christmas cookies that you may remember from your
childhood and some new ones to start your own traditions.

DECORATED CHRISTMAS CUTOUT COOKIES

I started making these cookies when I was a kid. It's been my go-to recipe for all occasions, especially at Christmastime. They are the perfect, delicate balance of crisp and chewy, and they were a favorite with my colleagues over the holidays. —L.K.

1 cup butter, softened

1 cup vegetable shortening

2 cups sugar

2 eggs, room temperature

2 teaspoons vanilla extract

4 cups flour

1 teaspoon salt

1 teaspoon baking soda

1 teaspoon cream of tartar

Royal Icing (see page 242)

In a medium mixing bowl, beat butter, shortening, sugar, eggs, and vanilla with a mixer for 1 to 2 minutes.

In a small mixing bowl, combine flour, salt, baking soda, and cream of tartar. Add to the butter mixture and beat just until combined.

Divide the dough in four portions. Wrap in plastic and refrigerate for 1 hour or overnight.

When ready to bake cookies, preheat oven to 350°F. On a floured surface, roll out one portion until it is about ¼ inch thick. Cut out shapes with your favorite cookie cutters.

Transfer cutouts to a cookie sheet. Leave about a 1-inch space between cookies. Bake for 10 to 12 minutes. Allow cookies to cool on the pan for 5 minutes before transferring them to a cooling rack.

After cookies have cooled completely, pipe decorations with Royal Icing. After icing has dried, store in a sealed container for up to 3 days or freeze for up to 3 months.

PREHEAT **350°F**   BAKE TIME: 10–12 MINUTES   *MAKES* **50**

I made these cookies every year when my kids were little. We used candy melts and paintbrushes to dress the gingerbread boys and girls. You can also decorate them with royal icing and try alternate shapes. —J.K.

½ cup butter, softened

½ cup vegetable shortening

1¼ cups brown sugar

1 egg, room temperature

1 teaspoon vanilla extract

¼ cup unsulphured molasses

3 cups flour

4 teaspoons Gingerbread Spice
    (see page 247) or 1½ teaspoons
    ground ginger, 1½ teaspoons
    cinnamon, ½ teaspoon ground
    cloves, and ½ teaspoon allspice

½ teaspoon salt

1 teaspoon baking soda

Royal Icing (see page 242)

In a medium mixing bowl, beat butter, shortening, brown sugar, egg, and vanilla with a mixer for 1 to 2 minutes. Add molasses and beat until combined.

In a small mixing bowl, combine flour, gingerbread spice, salt, and baking soda. Add to the butter mixture and beat just until combined.

Divide the dough into two portions. Wrap in plastic and refrigerate for 1 hour or overnight.

When ready to bake cookies, preheat oven to 325°F. On a floured surface, roll out one portion until it is about ¼ inch thick. Cut out shapes with your favorite cookie cutters. Repeat with second portion.

Transfer cutouts to a cookie sheet. Leave about a 1-inch space between cookies. Bake for 8 to 10 minutes. Allow cookies to cool on the pan for 5 minutes before transferring them to a cooling rack.

After cookies have cooled completely, pipe decorations with Royal Icing. After icing has dried, store in a sealed container for up to 5 days or freeze for up to 3 months.

PREHEAT **325°F**   BAKE TIME: 8-10 MINUTES   *MAKES* **36**

tip | The baking time on this recipe will yield a soft cookie with slightly crisp layer.
If you would prefer a more crisp cookie, increase baking time to 12 to 14 minutes.

BROWNED BUTTER
CUTOUT COOKIES

This cutout cookie is delicate and delicious with a rich, slightly nutty flavor from the browned butter. Be sure to refrigerate dough before rolling out so the butter has a chance to solidify.
—L.K.

2 cups butter

1 cup sugar

2 eggs, room temperature

1 tablespoon vanilla extract

4½ cups flour

1 teaspoon salt

2 teaspoon baking soda

Royal Icing (see page 242)

Set out a medium heatproof bowl near stove. Melt butter in a medium saucepan over medium heat. Whisk butter and continue to cook until small brown specs appear near the bottom of pan. Butter should have a nutty aroma. Remove from heat and pour into bowl to prevent further cooking and possibly burning butter. Refrigerate until butter has cooled completely.

In a medium mixing bowl, beat butter, sugar, eggs, and vanilla with a mixer for 1 to 2 minutes.

In a small mixing bowl, combine flour, salt, and baking soda. Add to the butter mixture and beat just until combined.

Divide the dough into two portions. Wrap in plastic and refrigerate for 1 hour or overnight.

When ready to bake cookies, preheat oven to 350°F. On a floured surface, roll out one portion until it is about ¼ inch thick. Cut out shapes with your favorite cookie cutters. Repeat with second portion.

Transfer cutouts to a cookie sheet. Leave about a 1-inch space between cookies. Bake for 10 to 12 minutes. Allow cookies to cool on the pan for 5 minutes before transferring them to a cooling rack.

After cookies have cooled completely, pipe decorations with Royal Icing. After icing has dried, store in a sealed container for up to 3 days or freeze for up to 3 months.

PREHEAT **350°F**   BAKE TIME: 10-12 MINUTES   *MAKES* **40**

This recipe is adapted from my childhood cutout cookie recipe. The cookies are richly chocolatey with a delicate, crisp texture. Though this is traditionally a Christmas recipe, I also love to pull this one out for decorated Halloween cookies. —L.K.

1 cup unsalted butter, softened

1 cup vegetable shortening

2 cups sugar

2 eggs, room temperature

2 teaspoons vanilla extract

1 cup (6 ounces) dark chocolate chips

3 cups flour

1 teaspoon salt

1 teaspoon baking soda

1 teaspoon cream of tartar

1 cup Dutch process cocoa

Royal Icing (see page 242)

Preheat oven to 350°F.

In a medium mixing bowl, beat butter, shortening, sugar, eggs, and vanilla with a mixer for 1 to 2 minutes.

In a heatproof bowl, melt chocolate chips in the microwave on low. Check and stir often. Be careful to heat only until the chips are melted. The melted chocolate should not be hot. Mix into the butter mixture.

In a small mixing bowl, combine flour, salt, baking soda, and cream of tartar. Sift in the cocoa. Add to the butter mixture and beat just until combined.

Divide the dough into four portions. On a floured surface, roll out one portion until it is about ¼ inch thick. Cut out your desired cookie shapes.

Transfer cutouts to a cookie sheet. Leave about 1 inch between cookies. Bake for 8 to 10 minutes. Allow cookies to cool on the pan for 5 minutes before transferring them to a cooling rack.

After cookies have cooled completely, pipe decorations with Royal Icing. After icing has dried, store in a sealed container for up to 3 days or freeze for up to 3 months.

PREHEAT **350°F** ✳ BAKE TIME: 8-10 MINUTES ✳ *MAKES* **50**

 tip If you have any difficulty working with the dough, you can refrigerate it for 30 minutes to get a firmer dough. If you leave the dough in the refrigerator for a longer time, let it set out for 30 minutes before working with it. The chocolate will make the dough very firm if it's refrigerated too long.

SOFT VANILLA COOKIES WITH BUTTERCREAM

Buttercream frosting is the ideal complement to these pillowy-soft, cake-like cookies. Pick your favorite buttercream flavor. This is a great cookie to get the kids involved with—add some food-coloring and sprinkles to make them festive and fun. —L.K.

½ **cup unsalted butter, softened**

4 **ounces cream cheese**

¼ **cup vegetable shortening**

1½ **cups sugar**

2 **eggs, room temperature**

2 **teaspoons vanilla extract**

3¼ **cups flour**

½ **teaspoon salt**

2 **teaspoons baking powder**

½ **batch buttercream of your choice (see pages 237–239)**

Sprinkles, optional

In a medium mixing bowl, beat butter, cream cheese, shortening, and sugar with a mixer until light and fluffy, about 3 minutes. Add eggs and vanilla and beat on high until combined.

In a small mixing bowl, combine flour, salt, and baking powder. Add to the butter mixture and beat just until combined.

Divide the dough into two portions. Cover in plastic wrap and refrigerate for 30 minutes, up to overnight.

When ready to bake, preheat oven to 350ºF. On a floured surface, roll out one portion until it is about ⅜ inch thick. This will be thicker than most rolled-out cookies. Cut out rounds with a 2½-inch cookie cutter. Repeat with second portion.

Transfer cutouts to a cookie sheet. Leave about 1½ inches between cookies. Bake for 12 to 15 minutes. Allow cookies to cool on the pan for 5 minutes before transferring them to a cooling rack.

After cookies have cooled completely, frost with your favorite buttercream and garnish with plenty of sprinkles. Store in a sealed container for up to 5 days.

PREHEAT **350°F**　　✳　BAKE TIME: 12–15 MINUTES　✳　　*MAKES* **36**

CEREAL M&M COOKIES

These are the first cookies I remember watching my mom mix up when I was a kid. They were favorites of mine, and now my son loves them. They are the perfect combination of chewy and crispy; they're great with chocolate chips, too. —L.K.

1 cup butter, softened

1 cup sugar

1 cup brown sugar

1 cup vegetable oil

1 egg, room temperature

1 tablespoon vanilla extract

3½ cups flour

1 teaspoon salt

1 teaspoon baking soda

1 cup old-fashioned oatmeal

1 cup cornflakes

3 cups M&M's

Preheat oven to 350°F.

In a medium mixing bowl, beat butter and sugars with a mixer for 3 minutes. Add oil, egg, and vanilla and beat until combined.

In a small mixing bowl, combine flour, salt, and baking soda. Add to the butter mixture and beat until combined.

Using a rubber spatula, stir in oatmeal, cornflakes, and M&M's.

Scoop dough onto cookie sheet with a cookie scoop, leaving 2 inches of space around each dough scoop. Bake until light brown, about 15 minutes. Allow cookies to cool on the pan for about 5 minutes before transferring them to a cooling rack.

Store in a sealed container for up to 5 days.

tip These cookies freeze nicely, and they taste great right out of the freezer.

PREHEAT **350°F** ✳ BAKE TIME: 15 MINUTES ✳ *MAKES* **48**

DARK CHOCOLATE CRINKLES

I love this Christmas classic even more with dark chocolate, which balances the sweet confectioners' sugar coating. They come out with a beautiful crinkled exterior and soft rich, middle. —L.K.

½ cup unsalted butter, softened

1 cup brown sugar

2 eggs, room temperature

2 teaspoons vanilla extract

1 cup (6 ounces) dark chocolate chips, 60% cacoa

1⅔ cups flour

¼ teaspoon salt

2 teaspoons baking powder

½ cup unsweetened cocoa

½ cup sugar, for coating

½–1 cup confectioners' sugar, for coating

In a medium mixing bowl, beat butter, brown sugar, eggs, and vanilla with a mixer for 1 to 2 minutes.

In a heatproof bowl, melt chocolate chips in the microwave on low. Check and stir often. Be careful to heat only until the chips are melted. The chocolate should not be hot, but if it is, allow it to cool before proceeding. Mix into the butter mixture.

In a small mixing bowl, combine flour, salt, and baking powder. Sift in the cocoa. Add to the butter mixture and beat just until combined.

Refrigerate dough for 1 hour (or more). The dough is difficult to handle at room temperature, so this step is essential.

When ready to bake, preheat oven to 350°F. Place each of the coating sugars in two separate bowls. Scoop refrigerated dough with a cookie scoop and roll into a ball. Coat the ball in sugar, and then generously coat it with confectioners' sugar.

Place coated dough ball on a cookie sheet and repeat, placing dough balls about 2 inches apart until the cookie sheet is full.

Bake for about 12 to 15 minutes. Allow the cookies to cool for about 5 minutes before transferring them to a cooling rack. Store in a sealed container for up to 5 days.

PREHEAT **350**°F　　✳　BAKE TIME: 12–15 MINUTES　✳　*MAKES* **36**

 tip | It's not essential that you dip the dough in granulated sugar first, but I've found that the cookies come out prettier if you do.

LEMON POPPY SEED STAMP COOKIES

Like a lemon poppy seed muffin in the form of a sweet and decorative cookie— these simple-to-make treats look and taste great for a cookie exchange or gathering.

COOKIE

1 cup unsalted butter, softened

¾ cup sugar

1 egg, room temperature

1 teaspoon vanilla extract

2 tablespoons lemon juice

Zest of 1 lemon

2½ cups flour

½ teaspoon salt

1 teaspoon baking powder

2 tablespoons poppy seeds

Sugar, for coating

GLAZE

2 tablespoons lemon juice

1 cup confectioners' sugar

Preheat oven to 350°F.

In a medium mixing bowl, beat butter and sugar until light and fluffy, about 3 minutes. Add egg, vanilla, and lemon juice and zest. Beat until combined.

In a small mixing bowl, combine flour, salt, baking powder, and poppy seeds. Add to the butter mixture and beat until combined.

Scoop dough with a cookie scoop and roll into a ball. Dip one half of the dough ball in sugar and place on a cookie sheet, sugar-side up. Center a cookie stamp on the ball and press until the dough reaches the edge of the stamp. The sugar should keep the dough from sticking to the stamp.

Bake until light brown at the edges, about 12 to 15 minutes. Allow cookies to cool on the pan for about 5 minutes before transferring them to a cooling rack.

While cookies are cooling, make glaze by mixing lemon juice and confectioners' sugar in a medium bowl. After cookies have cooled completely, coat tops with glaze using a pastry brush. Allow glaze to dry completely. Store in an airtight container for up to 5 days.

PREHEAT **350°F**   BAKE TIME: 12–15 MINUTES   *MAKES* **30**

tip | Cookie stamps are now commonly sold in craft stores and larger grocery stores in the cake decorating section.

ICEBOX COOKIES

Slice-and-bake cookies are fun to make in a variety of flavors. The base dough makes a simple, slightly crisp vanilla cookie. Try the variations on the next page for something different! Package these shortbread-like cookies in cupcake liners and box them up for a gift or a cookie swap. —L.K.

1 cup unsalted butter, softened

1 cup sugar

2 egg yolks

2 teaspoons vanilla extract

2¾ cups flour

½ teaspoon salt

½ teaspoon baking powder

½ teaspoon cream of tartar

Coarse sugar, for rolling, optional

In a medium mixing bowl, beat butter and sugar until light and fluffy, about 3 minutes. Add egg yolks and vanilla. Beat until combined.

In a small mixing bowl, combine flour, salt, baking powder, and cream of tartar. Add to the butter mixture and beat until combined. The dough will be quite dense.

Divide the dough in half and roll each portion into a log, about 2 inches in diameter. Sprinkle coarse sugar, if using, on counter and roll log in sugar until covered. Wrap each log in parchment or plastic wrap and refrigerate for an hour or up to 24 hours.

When ready to bake, preheat oven to 350°F. Remove one dough log from the refrigerator and place on a cutting board. Using a bread knife or other thin-bladed knife, slice dough about ¼ inch thick. Place on a baking sheet, leaving about 1 inch of space between dough slices.

Bake until light brown at the edges, about 10 minutes. Allow cookies to cool on the pan for about 5 minutes before transferring them to a cooling rack. Store in an airtight container for up to 5 days.

PREHEAT **350°F** | BAKE TIME: 10 MINUTES | *MAKES* **40**

TOFFEE

8 ounces milk chocolate English toffee bits

Add toffee at the end of the mixing process.

CHOCOLATE CHUNK

5 ounces semisweet chocolate, coarsely chopped

Add chocolate at the end of the mixing process.

WHITE CHOCOLATE PISTACHIO CRANBERRY

½ cup dried cranberries, chopped
½ cup pistachios, coarsely chopped
7 ounces white chocolate, coarsely chopped
¼ cup pistachios, finely chopped

Add cranberries and coarsely chopped pistachios at the end of the mixing process. After cookies have cooled completely, melt chocolate. Lay 2 feet of parchment on the counter. Dip half of each cookie in chocolate. Allow excess chocolate to drip off and set on parchment. Sprinkle with finely chopped pistachios before chocolate has a chance to set.

CHOCOLATE-COVERED CHERRY

20 maraschino cherries
3 tablespoons maraschino cherry juice
¼ cup flour
7 ounces bittersweet chocolate, coarsely chopped

Remove stems from cherries and discard. Chop coarsely. Add cherries, juice, and additional flour at the end of the mixing process. After cookies have cooled completely, melt chocolate. Lay 2 feet of parchment on the counter. Dip half of each cookie in chocolate. Allow excess chocolate to drip off and set on parchment.

CHOCOLATE HAZELNUT

4 ounces bittersweet chocolate, melted
2 tablespoons Dutch process cocoa
½ cup hazelnuts, coarsely chopped
2 ounces milk chocolate, coarsely chopped

Add melted chocolate to butter mixture before adding flour. Sift cocoa and add to flour mixture. Add hazelnuts at the end of the mixing process. After cookies have cooled completely, melt chocolate. Lay 2 feet of parchment on the counter. Set cookies close together on parchment. Drizzle chocolate over cookies with a fork using a fast diagonal motion.

CRANBERRY AND WHITE CHOCOLATE CHIP COOKIES

Sweet and festive, these soft, chewy cookies are fabulous right out of the oven. Try the alternate version with dark chocolate and toffee for more variety.

1 cup unsalted butter, softened

½ cup sugar

1 cup brown sugar

2 eggs, room temperature

1 tablespoon vanilla extract

2½ cups flour

1 teaspoon salt

1 teaspoon baking soda

¾ cup dried cranberries

2 cups white chocolate chips

1 cup pecans, coarsely chopped, optional

Preheat oven to 350°F.

In a medium mixing bowl, beat butter and sugars with a mixer for 3 minutes, until light and fluffy. Add eggs and vanilla and beat until combined.

In a small mixing bowl, combine flour, salt, and baking soda. Add to the butter mixture and beat until combined.

Using a rubber spatula, stir in cranberries, white chocolate chips, and pecans, if using.

Scoop dough onto cookie sheet with a cookie scoop, leaving 2 inches space around each scoop.

Bake just until cookies are light brown on edges but still gooey in the center, about 9 to 11 minutes. Allow cookies to cool on the pan for about 5 minutes before transferring them to a cooling rack. Store in an airtight container for up to 3 days or freeze for up to 3 months.

PREHEAT **350°F** * BAKE TIME: 9–11 MINUTES * *MAKES* **45**

variation

TOFFEE CHOCOLATE CHUNK COOKIES

8 ounces bittersweet chocolate, coarsely chopped
1½ cups toffee bits

Omit cranberries, white chocolate chips, and pecans. Mix in chocolate and toffee bits.

Cranberry and
White Chocolate
Chip Cookies

Toffee Chocolate
Chunk Cookies

Triple Chocolate
Peppermint Cookies

TRIPLE CHOCOLATE PEPPERMINT COOKIES

These cookies are loaded with chocolate and are gooey like a brownie—the peppermint adds the perfect holiday twist.

10 ounces bittersweet chocolate

1¼ cups butter (2½ sticks), softened

1 cup sugar

½ cup brown sugar

2 eggs, room temperature

1 tablespoon vanilla extract

2¼ cups flour

⅓ cup unsweetened cocoa

1 teaspoon salt

2 teaspoon baking powder

2 cups white chocolate peppermint chunks

2 cups dark chocolate chips

Preheat oven to 350°F.

In a heatproof bowl, melt chocolate in the microwave on low. Check and stir often. Be careful to heat only until the chocolate is melted. The chocolate should not be hot, but if it is, allow to cool before proceeding.

In a medium mixing bowl, beat butter and sugars with a mixer for 3 minutes, until light and fluffy. Add melted chocolate, eggs, and vanilla and beat until combined.

Sift flour, cocoa, salt, and baking powder into a small bowl and whisk to combine. Add to the butter mixture and beat until combined.

Using a rubber spatula, stir in white chocolate peppermint chunks and chocolate chips.

Scoop dough onto cookie sheet with a cookie scoop leaving 2 inches space around each scoop.

Bake just until cookies look crisp on edges but still gooey in the center, about 9 to 11 minutes. Allow cookies to cool on the pan for about 5 minutes before transferring them to a cooling rack. Once cookies are cool, store them in an airtight container for up to 5 days or freeze for up to 3 months.

PREHEAT **350°F** ✳ BAKE TIME: 9–11 MINUTES ✳ *MAKES* **50**

CHEWY GINGER MOLASSES COOKIES

These chewy cookies with the quintessential Christmas flavor of gingerbread spice are delightful with milk or coffee. Stack them in a large mason jar, tie on a bow, and they will make a cute Christmas gift.

¾ cup unsalted butter, softened

1 cup sugar

1 cup brown sugar

2 eggs, room temperature

2 teaspoons vanilla extract

⅓ cup unsulfured molasses

3½ cups flour

½ teaspoon salt

2 teaspoons baking soda

4 teaspoons Gingerbread Spice (see page 247) or 1½ teaspoons ground ginger, 1½ teaspoons cinnamon, ½ teaspoon ground cloves, and ½ teaspoon allspice

½ cup coarse sugar, for coating

Preheat oven to 350°F.

In a medium mixing bowl, beat butter, sugar, and brown sugar until light and fluffy, about 3 minutes. Add eggs, vanilla, and molasses. Beat until combined.

In a small bowl combine flour, salt, baking soda, and gingerbread spice. Add to the butter mixture and beat until combined.

Scoop dough with a cookie scoop and roll into a ball. Coat dough ball in coarse sugar and place on a cookie sheet. Leave 1½ inches of space between dough balls.

Bake 11 to 14 minutes. Allow cookies to cool on the pan for about 5 minutes before transferring them to a cooling rack. Store in an airtight container for up to a week.

PREHEAT **350°F** ✳ BAKE TIME: 11-14 MINUTES ✳ *MAKES* **36**

VANILLA MERINGUE COOKIES

These light-as-air beauties melt in your mouth, and you can customize the look with different piping tips and food coloring.

6 egg whites

1 teaspoon vanilla extract

½ teaspoon cream of tartar

¾ cup sugar

½ cup confectioners' sugar

Preheat oven to 200°F. Line a half-sheet pan with parchment or baking mat and set aside. Prepare a large piping bag with a large star or round tip and prop in a tall glass. Fold over the top 2 to 3 inches of the opening so it is ready to be filled.

In the bowl of a stand mixer with the whisk attachment, beat egg whites, vanilla, and cream of tartar at medium-low until foamy. Increase speed to medium, and add sugar and confectioners' sugar slowly, 1 teaspoon at a time. Increase speed to medium-high for 2 minutes. Increase again to high speed, and continue to beat until stiff peaks form, about 3 to 4 additional minutes.

With a rubber spatula, scoop meringue into prepared pastry bag. Pipe cookies in swirls or blobs onto the prepared baking sheet. Meringues do not expand like other cookies, so it's okay to space them about ¾ inch apart. Bake for 2 hours. After 2 hours, turn off the oven and leave them in the oven for another hour. This process is more about drying the meringues than baking them. Store meringues in an airtight container for up to 2 weeks.

PREHEAT **200°F**   BAKE TIME: 2 HOURS   *MAKES* **36**

variation

PEPPERMINT MERINGUE COOKIES

When preparing piping bag, paint 2 to 3 lines of pink or red food coloring from the tip to the fold inside the piping bag with a small paintbrush.

Replace vanilla extract with ½ teaspoon peppermint extract.

POMEGRANATE OATMEAL COOKIES

Pomegranates are plentiful over the holidays. I wanted to find a way to incorporate this healthy fruit in my holiday baking. These cookies are beauties and full of enough cereal, nuts, and fruit to be eaten for breakfast.

—L.K.

1 cup unsalted butter, softened

1 cup brown sugar

⅓ cup pure maple syrup, room temperature

2 eggs, room temperature

1 tablespoon vanilla extract

1¾ cups flour

1 teaspoon salt

1 teaspoon cinnamon

1 teaspoon baking soda

3 cups old-fashioned oatmeal

1 cup pecans, coarsely chopped

1 cup fresh pomegranate seeds

Maple Glaze (see page 234), optional

Preheat oven to 350°F.

In a medium mixing bowl, beat butter and brown sugar with a mixer until light and fluffy, about 3 minutes. Add maple syrup, eggs, and vanilla and beat until combined.

In a small mixing bowl, combine flour, salt, cinnamon, and baking soda. Add to the butter mixture and beat until combined.

Using a rubber spatula, stir in oatmeal, pecans, and pomegranate seeds.

Scoop dough onto cookie sheet with cookie scoop, leaving 2 to 3 inches of space around each dough scoop.

Bake until light brown, about 15 minutes. Allow cookies to cool on the pan for about 5 minutes before transferring them to a cooling rack. Allow to cool completely before storing or adding glaze.

If using maple glaze, place parchment below cooling rack. Place cookies as close together on the rack as possible and drizzle with glaze. Allow glaze to dry for about 30 minutes before storing in an airtight container for up to 1 week.

PREHEAT **350°F**   ✦   BAKE TIME: 14–17 MINUTES   ✦   *MAKES* **36**

PEANUT BUTTER BLOSSOMS

In the Midwest, this cookie is an essential at Christmas and is often made year-round. Peanut butter and chocolate are a winning combination. This version is extra peanut buttery.

½ cup unsalted butter, softened

1 cup brown sugar

¾ cup (6.6 ounces) peanut butter

1 egg, room temperature

2 teaspoons vanilla extract

1¾ cups flour

½ teaspoon salt

1 teaspoon baking soda

½ cup sugar, for coating

30 Hershey's Kisses

Preheat oven to 350°F.

In a medium mixing bowl, beat butter, brown sugar, and peanut butter until light and fluffy, about 4 minutes. Add egg and vanilla. Beat until combined.

In a small bowl, combine flour, salt, and baking soda. Add to the butter mixture and beat until combined.

Scoop dough with a cookie scoop and roll into a ball. Coat dough ball in sugar and place on a cookie sheet. Leave 1½ inches of space between dough balls.

Bake 10 to 12 minutes. Immediately after removing cookies from oven, press one Hershey's Kiss into the center of each still-hot cookie. Press about ¼ to ½ inch into the cookie—just far enough for the Kiss to attach but not so far that the cookie is flattened. Allow cookies to cool on the pan for about 5 minutes before transferring them to a cooling rack.

Once cookies are cool, store them in an airtight container for up to 5 days.

PREHEAT **350°F**   BAKE TIME: 10–12 MINUTES   MAKES **30**

tip | If you want to change up this recipe a bit, try Hershey's Hugs or Brach's Chocolate Stars in place of Hershey's Kisses.

SHORTBREAD

I don't think there's any shortbread better than what you'll find in Scotland. This recipe is the closest I've found to replicating the flaky, buttery, amazing taste of Scottish shortbread. Don't skip the extra-long time beating the butter and sugar; it adds air to the dough and will produce the best results. —L.K.

1½ cups butter, softened

¾ cups superfine sugar

1 tablespoon vanilla extract

2½ cups flour

½ teaspoon salt

2 tablespoons sugar

Yummy ☺

Preheat oven to 300°F. Line a quarter-sheet pan or 9-by-13-inch pan with parchment and set aside.

In the bowl of a stand mixer with the paddle attachment, beat butter and sugar on high for about 10 minutes. About halfway through the mixing time, stop to scrape down the sides and bottom of the bowl to ensure even mixing. Add vanilla and beat until combined.

In a small bowl, mix flour and salt. Add to butter mixture and beat until combined. Press dough evenly into prepared pan. Sprinkle with 2 tablespoons sugar. Bake for about 1 hour or until lightly golden.

While shortbread is still hot, create a pattern with the tines of a fork. Press fork about ⅛ inch into top of shortbread. Make 2 cuts on the long side to make 3 long pieces. Cut 10 cuts on the short side for a total of 33 pieces. This works best while the shortbread is still hot. After cutting, leave shortbread in pan to cool. Shortbread may crumble if removed while hot.

Store in an airtight container for up to a week or freeze for up to 3 months.

PREHEAT **300°F**   BAKE TIME: 1 HOUR   *MAKES* **33**

CHOCOLATE SHORTBREAD

Chocolate shortbread is a fabulous, rich accompaniment to coffee. A batch fits neatly into a box and makes a great gift for anyone who likes a little sweetness with their afternoon cup of joe.

1½ cups butter, softened

1 cups superfine sugar

1 teaspoon vanilla extract

⅓ cup Dutch process cocoa

2¼ cups flour

½ teaspoon salt

1 teaspoon espresso powder, optional

2 tablespoons sugar

Preheat oven to 300°F. Line a quarter-sheet pan or 9-by-13-inch pan with parchment and set aside.

In the bowl of a stand mixer with the paddle attachment, beat butter and sugar on high for about 10 minutes. About halfway through the mixing time, stop to scrape down the sides and bottom of the bowl to ensure even mixing. Add vanilla and beat until combined.

In a small bowl, mix cocoa, flour, salt, and espresso powder, if using. Add to butter mixture and beat until combined. Press dough evenly into prepared pan. Sprinkle with 2 tablespoons sugar. Bake for about 55 minutes.

While shortbread is still hot, create a pattern with the tines of a fork. Press fork about ⅛ inch into top of shortbread. Make 2 cuts on the long side to make 3 long pieces. Cut 10 cuts on the short side for a total of 33 pieces. This works best while the shortbread is still hot. After cutting, leave shortbread in pan to cool. Shortbread may crumble if removed while hot.

Store in an airtight container for up to a week or freeze for up to 3 months.

PREHEAT **300°F**   BAKE TIME: 55 MINUTES   *MAKES* **33**

CRACKER DATE COOKIES

I love to make plates with a variety of goodies to share with friends at Christmastime. This is one of my favorites to include. —J.K.

COOKIE
16 ounces chopped dates
1 cup chopped pecans
1 can sweetened condensed milk
2 sleeves Ritz crackers

FROSTING
½ cup unsalted butter, softened
4 cups confectioners' sugar
1 teaspoon vanilla extract
1–2 tablespoons milk

Preheat oven to 350°F.

To make cookies: Fill a cookie sheet with a single layer of Ritz crackers and set aside.

In a medium saucepan over medium heat, cook dates, pecans, and condensed milk until thickened. Spread 1 tablespoon of the mixture onto each cracker. Bake for 6 minutes.

Allow to cool completely.

To make the frosting: In a medium bowl, beat all frosting ingredients on high for 2 to 3 minutes. Frost cooled cookies. Store in an airtight container for up to 1 week.

PREHEAT **350°F**   BAKE TIME: 6 MINUTES   *MAKES* **70**

CRANBERRY THUMBPRINTS

Classic thumbprints are made by making an indent in a dough ball with your thumb and filling it with jam. You can also use specialty thumbprint cookie cutters for a fancier look. These are delicious either way.

1 cup unsalted butter, softened

1¼ cups sugar

2 eggs, room temperature

1 teaspoon vanilla extract

1 teaspoon almond extract

3½ cups flour

½ teaspoon salt

1 teaspoon baking powder

½ cup Cranberry Almond Jam (see page 231)

Preheat oven to 350°F.

In a medium mixing bowl, beat butter and sugar until light and fluffy, about 3 minutes. Add eggs, vanilla, and almond extract. Beat until combined.

In a small mixing bowl, combine flour, salt, and baking powder. Add to the butter mixture and beat until combined.

Scoop dough with a cookie scoop and roll into a ball. Place on a baking sheet, press thumb into the ball, and create a ½-inch indent. Fill indent with jam. Leave at least 1 inch of space between dough balls.

If using thumbprint cookie cutters, roll out dough on a lightly floured surface. Make cutouts and transfer to baking sheet, leaving at least 1 inch of space between each. Fill indents with jam.

Bake until light brown at the edges, about 12 to 14 minutes. Allow cookies to cool on the pan for about 5 minutes before transferring them to a cooling rack.

Once cookies are cool, store them in an airtight container for up to 5 days.

PREHEAT **350°F** ✳ BAKE TIME: 12–14 MINUTES ✳ *MAKES* **36**

Sandwich cookies are double the fun and make a great gift. Pick your favorite buttercream to complement these dark chocolate cookies.

½ cup (3 ounces) dark chocolate chips

1 cup unsalted butter, softened

1 cup sugar

2 eggs, room temperature

2 teaspoons vanilla extract

2 cups flour

½ teaspoon salt

½ teaspoon baking soda

½ cup unsweetened cocoa

½ batch buttercream of your choice (see pages 237–239)

Preheat oven to 350°F.

In a heatproof bowl, melt chocolate chips in the microwave on low. Check and stir often. Be careful to heat only until the chips are melted. The chocolate should not be hot, but if it is, allow to cool before proceeding.

In a medium mixing bowl, beat butter, sugar, eggs, vanilla, and melted chocolate with a mixer for 3 minutes.

In a small bowl, combine flour, salt, and baking soda. Sift the cocoa into flour mixture. Add to the butter mixture and beat just until combined.

Divide the dough in half. On a floured surface, roll out one portion until it is about ¼-inch thick. Make cutouts with a 1¾-inch-round cookie cutter. Repeat with second portion.

Transfer cutouts to a cookie sheet. Leave about a 1-inch space between cookies. Bake for 8 to 10 minutes. Allow cookies to cool on the pan for 5 minutes before transferring them to a cooling rack.

After cookies have cooled completely, spread buttercream on a cookie and top with a second cookie. Twist until buttercream reaches the edges of the cookies.

Store in an airtight container for up to 5 days. Over time, the cookies will absorb the moisture from the buttercream. For crisp cookies, assemble the cookies just before serving.

PREHEAT **350°F** · BAKE TIME: 8-10 MINUTES · *MAKES* **40**

CHAPTER

2

International
COOKIES

COOKIES FROM AROUND THE WORLD

make excellent additions to your holiday baking repertoire. Many of these are already considered Christmas classics, and some may be new to you. Try a few of these the next time you go to a cookie swap party or when baking up gifts for family and friends. A festive box filled with an array of cookie flavors is a treat and seasonal joy.

These almond and meringue–based confections have been popular in France for centuries and were converted to their current sandwich form in Parisian bakeries. Now macarons come in every imaginable flavor and color. This red velvet version is perfect for Christmas and makes an elegant gift.

SHELLS

⅔ cup almond flour

1 cup confectioners' sugar

2 teaspoons Dutch process cocoa

¼ teaspoon salt

2 egg whites

¼ cup sugar

10 drops red gel food coloring

FILLING

2 tablespoons unsalted butter

4 ounces cream cheese

½ teaspoon vanilla extract

1¼ cups confectioners' sugar

Milk, optional

Line a half-sheet baking pan with parchment or nonstick baking mat and set aside. Prepare a large piping bag with a medium round tip and prop in a tall glass. Fold over the top 2 to 3 inches of the opening so it is ready to be filled.

Sift almond flour, confectioners' sugar, and cocoa into a medium mixing bowl. Whisk in salt and mix until incorporated. Set aside.

In the bowl of a stand mixer with the whisk attachment, beat egg whites at medium-low speed until foamy. Increase speed to medium and add sugar slowly, 1 teaspoon at a time. Increase speed to medium-high for 2 minutes. Increase again to high speed and continue to beat until stiff peaks form, about 2 to 4 additional minutes. Add gel food coloring and turn mixer on low just until color is incorporated.

Add the dry ingredients to the meringue. Fold together with a rubber spatula. The longer the ingredients are mixed, the more deflated the egg whites will get, and the batter will become runnier. This step is one of the most crucial aspects of getting your macaron shells to come out right. When the batter falls off the spatula in ribbons, it is ready. One way to check is to try to draw a figure eight with the batter without the batter breaking. Once you're able to do this, stop mixing and pour into the prepared piping bag.

(continued)

Pipe circles onto the prepared baking sheet. Hold the piping bag vertical and the tip close to the baking sheet. Create rounds about 1¾ inches wide; these will spread to about 2 inches. Make 5 rows of 4 for a total of 20. Specialty baking mats for macarons are helpful to size and space batter. Tap the pan on the counter several times to release air bubbles.

Allow the pan to rest for 30 to 60 minutes until the outside of macaron shells have dried. You should be able to lightly touch the shell without it sticking to your finger. It's tempting to skip this step, but it is essential to getting the macaron shells to rise properly. Preheat oven to 300°F. Bake shells for 17 minutes. Don't open the oven door while baking. After removing from oven, allow the shells to rest on the pan for 30 minutes before removing them. This will allow the bottoms to dry completely and make them easy to lift off the parchment or baking mat.

While cooling, make filling. Using a stand mixer with the paddle attachment, beat the butter, cream cheese, vanilla, and confectioners' sugar for 5 minutes, until fluffy. Scrape the bowl, including the bottom, to make sure all ingredients are being incorporated. If buttercream is too thick, you can add milk 1 teaspoon at a time.

Prepare a medium piping bag with a medium round tip and prop in a tall glass. Fold over the top 2 to 3 inches of the opening and fill with cream cheese frosting. Once macaron shells are completely cooled, pipe frosting onto one shell and top with another to form a sandwich. Continue with remaining shells. Store macarons in an airtight container for up to 1 week.

PREHEAT **300°F**   BAKE TIME: 17 MINUTES   *MAKES* **10**

DUTCH WINDMILL COOKIES

Growing up in a Dutch community, windmill cookies were a staple of my childhood. They can be rolled out and cut with cookie cutters or flattened with a cookie stamp. —J.K.

1½ cups unsalted butter

1⅓ cups dark brown sugar

3 tablespoons milk

3 cups flour

½ teaspoon salt

1 tablespoon cinnamon

½ teaspoon ground cloves

1½ teaspoons nutmeg

1 teaspoon baking soda

Sliced almonds, optional

Preheat oven 350°F.

In a medium mixing bowl, beat butter and brown sugar until light and fluffy, about 3 minutes. Add milk and beat until combined.

In a small mixing bowl, combine flour, salt, cinnamon, ground cloves, nutmeg, and baking soda. Add to the butter mixture and beat until combined.

Divide the dough in half. On a lightly floured surface, roll out one portion of dough to about ¼-inch thickness. Cut out shapes with your favorite cookie cutters. Repeat with the second portion of dough.

Transfer cutouts to a cookie sheet. Leave about a 1-inch space between cookies. Top cookies with sliced almonds, if using. Bake for 11 to 13 minutes. Allow cookies to cool on the pan for 5 minutes before transferring them to a cooling rack.

Once cookies are cool, store them in an airtight container for up to 5 days or freeze for up to 3 months.

PREHEAT **350°F** ✳ BAKE TIME: 11–13 MINUTES ✳ *MAKES* **30**

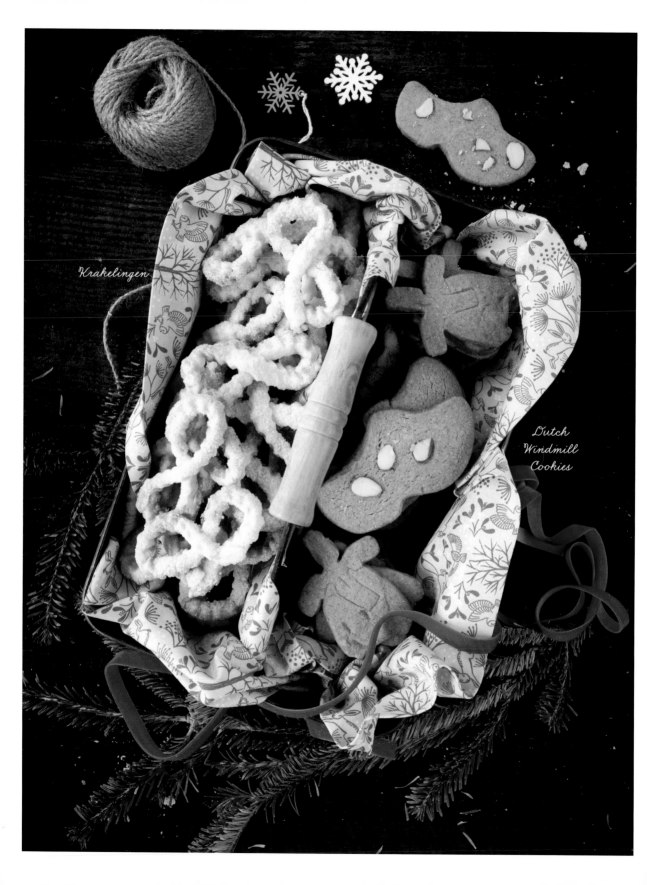

Krakelingen

Dutch
Windmill
Cookies

This melt-in-your-mouth, delicious Dutch cookie is a favorite at parties and gatherings. It is as simple to make as piecrust but rolled out with sugar instead of flour.

2 cups flour

½ teaspoon salt

1 cup unsalted butter

¼–½ cup ice water

½–¾ sugar, for rolling

tip | It is important to get the dough rolled out to close to the desired size. Unlike other doughs, it can't be rolled a second time, as the proportion of sugar will become too high on a second rollout.

In a medium bowl, mix the flour and salt. Slice the butter into small pats and toss into the flour. Cut the butter and flour with a pastry blender until you have a fine crumb. This step can also be achieved with a food processor. Be careful not to overprocess.

Turn out the crumb mixture on a pastry board or counter. Sprinkle ¼ cup of the ice water over the crumb mixture. Combine with your hands, squeezing the crumbs together until a dough forms. If the dough doesn't come together, add more ice water 1 tablespoon at a time until you get the dough to form.

Flatten dough into a rectangle, roughly 8 by 4 inches. Cover with plastic wrap. Refrigerate for 1 hour or up to 12 hours.

When ready to roll out the dough, preheat oven to 350°F. Evenly spread ¼ cup of sugar on an 8-by-16-inch space on a pastry board or counter. Place the dough rectangle in the center of the sugar. Sprinkle the top of the dough with more sugar. Roll the dough until it is about ¼-inch thick, forming a rough rectangle about 8 by 16 inches. Add more sugar to the top as you roll to prevent the rolling pin from sticking and to form an even layer of sugar on the dough. Check the bottom of the dough and add sugar in any spots that do not have any.

Using a pastry wheel or pizza cutter, cut ¼-inch strips off the 8-inch side of the dough rectangle. Form a circle with one strip. Pinch the ends together to connect. Make one twist in the circle to make a figure eight and place on baking sheet, spacing about 1 inch apart.

Bake for 15 to 20 minutes or until a light golden brown. Store in an airtight container for up to a week or freeze for up to 3 months.

PREHEAT **350°F**   BAKE TIME: 15–20 MINUTES   *MAKES* **50**

Banket is a sweet almond-paste pastry that originated in the Netherlands and is a popular Christmas treat for many Dutch families. Gifting banket by wrapping in parchment and tying with a ribbon is a tradition in in our family and the Dutch community.

PASTRY

2 cups flour

½ teaspoon salt

1 cup unsalted butter

½ cup ice water + more if needed

FILLING

8 ounces almond paste

1 egg

1 cups granulated sugar

1½ teaspoons lemon juice

½ teaspoon almond extract

EGG WASH

1 egg white

¼ cup coarse sugar

To make the pastry: In a medium bowl, mix the flour and salt. Slice the butter into small pats and toss into the flour. Cut the butter and flour with a pastry blender until you have a fine crumb. This step can also be achieved with a food processor. Be careful not to overprocess.

Turn out the crumb mixture on a pastry board or counter. Sprinkle ½ cup of ice water over the crumb mixture. Combine with your hands, squeezing the crumbs together until a dough forms. If the dough doesn't come together, add more ice water 1 teaspoon at a time until you get the dough to form. Divide dough into 2 portions and flatten into a rectangular shape. Cover with plastic wrap and refrigerate for 4 hours, up to overnight.

To make the filling: Grate the almond paste into a mixing bowl. Add egg, sugar, lemon juice, and almond extract. Beat until well combined. Pour into a sealable plastic bowl. Cover and freeze 4 hours, up to overnight.

When ready to bake, preheat oven to 425°F.

Line a half-sheet baking pan with parchment or a baking mat and set aside.

Beat egg white and set aside.

(continued)

PREHEAT **425°**F
REDUCE TO **350°**F

BAKE TIME: 10 MINUTES
& 15–18 MINUTES

MAKES **4** LOGS

Roll out one portion of dough to approximately 12 by 14 inches. Cut in half lengthwise for two 6 by 14 inch pieces.

Cut almond paste filling into 4 portions. Coat hands in flour and roll one portion of almond paste into a log a little shorter than dough.

Place almond paste in center of dough. Use a bench scraper to loosen dough from pastry board.

Roll the dough around almond paste, loosely. Tuck in ends.

Carefully place seam-side down on baking sheet. Repeat with second half of dough.

Brush dough logs with egg wash, coating top and sides.

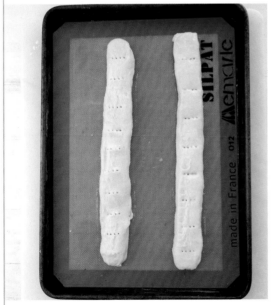

Poke holes in the top with a fork every 2 inches. Don't skip this step or rolls might burst.

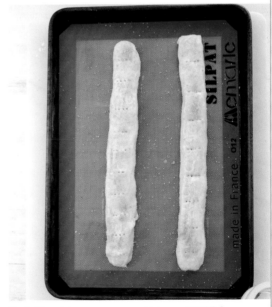

Sprinkle with coarse sugar. Bake at 425°F for 10 minutes Turn oven down to 350°F and continue baking for 15 to 18 additional minutes or until light brown.

MEXICAN WEDDING COOKIES

Known as *polvorones* in Mexico, these delicate domes of buttery sweetness have become common at Christmas in the United States and are an excellent addition to cookie swap parties or for sharing in a mixed cookie gift box.

1 cup unsalted butter

⅔ cup confectioners' sugar, plus more for coating

2 teaspoons vanilla extract

2 cups flour

1 teaspoon cinnamon

½ teaspoon salt

1 cup walnuts

Preheat oven to 350°F. Beat butter, sugar, and vanilla for about 3 minutes until light and fluffy.

In a medium bowl, whisk together flour, cinnamon, and salt. Add to the butter mixture and beat until well combined.

Using a food processer, chop the walnuts until they are fine. Add to the dough and beat until completely incorporated. Form 1-inch balls from the dough and place on a cookie sheet, leaving 1 to 2 inches between each dough ball. Bake for 15 to 18 minutes.

While cookies bake, add about 1 cup of confectioners' sugar to a bowl. After cookies are out of the oven, allow them to cool for about 3 minutes. Scoop each cookie into the confectioners' sugar one at a time. It's important that the cookies are still somewhat hot for this step, as is helps the confectioners' sugar stick to the cookie. Place the covered cookies on a cooling rack to cool completely. Store in an airtight container for up to 5 days.

PREHEAT **350°**F *BAKE TIME: 15–18 MINUTES* *MAKES* **36**

Alfajores consist of two airy cookies made extra light from a generous amount of cornstarch sandwiching dulce de leche. These luscious sandwich cookies are popular throughout South America, especially in Argentina.

1 cup unsalted butter

¾ cup sugar

1 tablespoon vanilla extract

3 egg yolks, room temperature

1½ cups flour

1⅔ cups cornstarch

2 teaspoons baking powder

½ teaspoon salt

1½ cups Dulce de Leche (see page 233)

½ cup shredded sweetened coconut, opitonal

Confectioners' sugar for dusting, optional

Beat butter, sugar, and vanilla for 2 to 3 minutes until fluffy. Add egg yolks and beat until combined.

In a medium bowl, whisk together flour, cornstarch, baking powder, and salt. Add to the butter mixture and beat until well combined.

Divide the dough into two portions. Wrap each portion in plastic and refrigerate for 30 minutes, up to overnight.

When ready to bake, preheat oven to 350°F. On a floured surface, roll out one portion until it is about ¼-inch thick. Cut out rounds with a 2-inch cookie cutter. Repeat with second portion.

Transfer cutouts to a cookie sheet. Leave about 1½ inches between cookies. Bake for 10 to 12 minutes. Allow cookies to cool on the pan for 5 minutes before transferring them to a cooling rack.

After cookies have cooled completely, spread dulce de leche on a cookie and top with a second cookie. Roll sides in coconut and dust with confectioners' sugar, if using.

Store in an airtight container for up to 5 days. Over time, the cookies will absorb the moisture from the dulce de leche. For crisp cookies, assemble the cookies just before serving.

PREHEAT **350°F** ✳ BAKE TIME: 10–12 MINUTES ✳ *MAKES* **25**

tip | If you don't have time to make homemade dulce de leche, there are many excellent jarred varieties available to purchase.

NANKHATAI

Rose water and cardamom set these Pakistani shortbread cookies apart from a typical American cookie. I've altered the recipe to make it easier to make from an American pantry, but the original flavors remain. My friend tested them and assured me that they brought back memories of growing up in Karachi and the pretty little boxes her family brought home from the bakery. —L.K.

COOKIE
1 cup unsalted butter

1 cup sugar

1 teaspoon rose water

1 egg yolk

2½ cups flour

½ teaspoon baking soda

¼ teaspoon salt

1 teaspoon ground cardamom

TOPPING
1 egg

½ cup pistachios, finely chopped

Edible rose petals for garnish, optional

Preheat oven to 350°F. Beat butter, sugar, and rose water for 3 minutes until light and fluffy. Add egg yolk to the butter mixture and beat until combined.

In a medium bowl, whisk together flour, baking soda, salt, and cardamom. Add to the butter mixture and beat until well combined.

Scoop dough and form 1-inch balls and place on a baking tray. Leave 1½ to 2 inches between dough balls. Lightly press down on each ball so it is about ¾ of its original height.

In a medium bowl, beat egg with a wire whisk until foamy. Using a pastry brush, coat the cookies with egg wash. Sprinkle with pistachios.

Bake for 14 to 16 minutes or until light golden brown. Allow to cool on the pan for 5 minutes before transferring to a cool rack. Allow to cool completely and then store in an airtight container for up to 1 week.

Garnish with rose petals, if using, just before serving.

PREHEAT **350°F**   BAKE TIME: 14–16 MINUTES   *MAKES* **36**

Champurradas are common throughout Guatemala and are a traditional accompaniment to afternoon coffee. These sesame seed cookies are crunchy and perfect for dunking in coffee or hot chocolate. With two Guatemalans in my household, they are a favorite to have in the cookie jar. —L.K.

1 cup shortening

1 cup sugar

1 tablespoon vanilla extract

3 eggs, divided

3½ cups flour

1 teaspoon baking powder

1 teaspoon salt

1½ teaspoons milk

2 tablespoons sesame seeds

Preheat oven to 350°F. Beat shortening, sugar, and vanilla for 2 to 3 minutes until fluffy. Add 2 eggs. Separate the yolk and egg white of the third egg. Add the yolk to the shortening mixture and reserve the egg white for later.

In a medium bowl, whisk together flour, baking powder, and salt. Add to the shortening mixture and beat until well combined.

On a lightly floured surface, roll out half the dough to ¼-inch thickness. Cut out 3½-inch rounds with a cookie cutter and place on a cookie sheet.

In a medium bowl, beat reserved egg white with a wire whisk until foamy. Add milk. Using a pastry brush, coat the cookies with egg wash. Sprinkle with sesame seeds. Bake for 14 to 16 minutes or until light golden brown. Allow cookies to cool on the pan for 5 minutes before transferring them to a cooling rack.

Store in an airtight container for up to 1 week.

PREHEAT **350°F**   BAKE TIME: 14-16 MINUTES   *MAKES* **24**

Originating from Jewish communities in Poland, rugelach has a lightly crisp, flaky crust with fruit and nuts rolled into a crescent shape. This version also has chocolate and will be a popular addition to your holiday cookie trays.

CRUST

2 cups flour

½ teaspoon salt

8 ounces cream cheese

1 cup butter

¼ cup buttermilk

FILLING

½ cup brown sugar

½ cup pecans, finely chopped

⅓ cup dried cherries, finely chopped

1 teaspoon cinnamon

1 cup mini semisweet chocolate chips

TOPPING

1 egg

¼ coarse sugar, for sprinkling

In a medium bowl, mix the flour and salt. Slice cream cheese and butter into small pats and toss into the flour. Cut cream cheese, butter, and flour with a pastry blender until you have a fine crumb. This step can also be achieved with a food processor. Be careful not to overprocess.

Turn out the crumb mixture on a pastry board or counter. Sprinkle buttermilk over the crumb mixture. Combine with your hands, squeezing the crumbs together until a dough forms. Divide dough into 3 parts. Flatten each portion into a disk. Cover with plastic wrap. Refrigerate for 1 hour or up to 12 hours.

When ready to roll out the dough, preheat oven to 350° F. Line baking sheet with parchment or a baking mat and set aside.

Combine filling ingredients and set aside. Roll out one disk of dough into a 10-inch circle. Sprinkle one third of the filling over the dough, going all the way to the edge. Lightly press down on filling so it sticks to the dough. With a pizza cutter, make 6 cuts to create 12 equal wedges. Starting from the wide side of a wedge, roll and place on prepared baking sheet. (See next page for photographic instructions.)

Beat egg and brush onto rolled dough. Sprinkle with coarse sugar. Bake 20 to 25 minutes until golden brown. Serve warm or cool and store in an airtight container for up to 3 days. Freeze for up to 3 months.

PREHEAT **350°**F　　✳　BAKE TIME: 20–25 MINUTES　✳　　*MAKES* **36**

Combine filling ingredients.

Roll out one disk of dough into a 10-inch circle.

Sprinkle one third of filling over dough, going all the way to edge. Lightly press down on the filling so it sticks to the dough.

Starting from the wide side of a wedge, roll and place on prepared baking sheet.

KOLACZKI

These flaky cream cheese and jam cookies are traditionally made in Poland for the holidays. You can replace the raspberry jam with any jam you prefer or use different flavors for a variety of cookies.

8 ounces cream cheese, softened

1½ cups butter, softened

¼ cup sugar

1 teaspoon vanilla extract

½ teaspoon almond extract

3 cups flour

½ teaspoon salt

½ cup Raspberry Jam (see page 230)

Confectioners' sugar for dusting

In a mixing bowl, beat cream cheese, butter, sugar, vanilla, and almond extract for 3 to 4 minutes, until light and fluffy.

In a small bowl, combine flour and salt. Add to cream cheese mixture and beat until combined.

Divide dough in half. Flatten each portion into a disk. Cover with plastic wrap. Refrigerate for 1 hour or up to 12 hours.

When ready to roll out the dough, preheat oven to 350°F. Line baking sheet with parchment or a baking mat and set aside.

Roll out dough to ¼-inch thick. Cut out 2½-inch squares. Place square on baking sheet. Spread about 2 teaspoons jam on the square. Fold two opposite corners over and press together. Bake 12 to 16 minutes. Allow cookies to cool on the pan for about 5 minutes before transferring them to a cooling rack. Dust with confectioners' sugar, if using.

Store in an airtight container for up to 1 week.

PREHEAT **350°F** ✳ BAKE TIME: 12–16 MINUTES ✳ *MAKES* **46**

These elegant little beauties are named for the linzer torte from Linz, Austria. The toasted ground almonds give the cookie a unique texture that pairs nicely with the sweet jam. Use a specially designed linzer cookie cutter or a tiny cutter to make the little windows that show off the raspberry jam.

½ cup almonds

1 cup unsalted butter

1 cup sugar

1 teaspoon vanilla extract

2 egg yolks, room temperature

2¼ cups flour

1 teaspoon baking powder

½ teaspoon salt

½ teaspoon cinnamon

Confectioners' sugar for dusting
1 cup Raspberry Jam (see page 230)

Preheat oven to 350°F. Place almonds on a single layer on a baking sheet, bake 7 minutes, and allow to cool.

Beat butter, sugar, and vanilla for 2 to 3 minutes until fluffy. Add egg yolks and beat until combined.

In food processor, process cooled almonds until fine. Add flour, baking powder, salt, and cinnamon. Pulse until well combined. Add flour mixture to the butter mixture and beat until well combined.

Divide the dough into two portions. Wrap each portion in plastic and refrigerate for 30 minutes, up to overnight.

When ready to bake, preheat oven to 350°F. On a floured surface, roll out one portion until it is about ¼ inch thick. Cut out rounds with a 2-inch cookie cutter. Cut small shape windows in half of the cutouts. Repeat with second portion,

Transfer cutouts to a cookie sheet. Leave about 1½ inches between cookies. Bake for 10 to 14 minutes. Allow cookies to cool on the pan for 5 minutes before transferring them to a cooling rack.

After cookies have cooled completely, dust the cookies with window cutouts with confectioners' sugar. Spread raspberry jam on a bottom cookie and top with window cookie. Over time, the cookies will absorb the moisture from the jam. For crisp cookies, assemble the cookies just before serving.

PREHEAT **350°F**   BAKE TIME: 10-14 MINUTES   *MAKES* **32**

MINT CHOCOLATE CHIP BISCOTTI

The word *biscotti* derives from Latin *biscoctus,* meaning "twice-baked." This version of the crunchy Italian, dip-able cookie is a festive addition to afternoon coffee or tea. Biscotti are also perfect for care packages, as they remain fresh much longer than a typical cookie.

5 tablespoons unsalted butter, softened

1 cup sugar

3 eggs, room temperature

1 teaspoon peppermint extract

2½ cups flour

½ teaspoon salt

1 tablespoon baking powder

3 drops green gel food coloring

1 cup mini chocolate chips

6 ounces milk chocolate

Preheat oven to 375°F. Line a half-sheet baking tray with parchment or a baking mat.

In a medium mixing bowl, beat butter and sugar with a mixer for 3 minutes, until light and fluffy. Add eggs and peppermint extract and beat until combined.

In a small mixing bowl, combine flour, salt, and baking powder. Add to the butter mixture and beat until combined. Add green food coloring and mix until green is evenly distributed. Stir in chocolate chips.

Divide dough in half. With floured hands, form each half into a log that is about the length of the baking sheet. Place both logs on the prepared pan. Bake 30 minutes.

Remove from oven and let rest for 5 to 10 minutes. Reduce oven temperature to 325°F. Prepare a second baking pan, placing a cooling rack on top of a baking pan. Slice biscotti logs on an angle into ½-inch to ¾-inch slices. Place slices on side on cooling rack. Biscotti will not expand on second baking, so you can place them close together.

Bake second time for 20 minutes. Allow to cool completely.

Lay out 2 to 3 feet of parchment on counter. Melt milk chocolate. Dip one third of each biscotti in chocolate and set on parchment to dry. After chocolate has set completely, store in an airtight container for up to 3 weeks.

PREHEAT **375°F**
REDUCE TO **325°F**

BAKE TIME: 30 MINUTES & 20 MINUTES

MAKES **40**

CHAPTER

3

FROM GOOEY CARAMEL TO RICH CHOCOLATE,

bars are a decadent addition to holiday baking. One pan makes them simple to prepare and easy to take with you to share at work or a party. Eat them warm straight from the pan or turn them into a dessert by topping them with ice cream—either way, your family and friends will be thrilled.

ALMOND TOFFEE BARS

I love toffee, and these shortbread-like bars are my favorite. They are easy to make and richly delicious. Bring a tray to a party or share in a gift box. —L.K.

¾ cups almonds, divided

1½ cups unsalted butter

1½ cups brown sugar

½ cup sugar

1 tablespoon vanilla extract

3 cups flour

1 teaspoon baking powder

½ teaspoon salt

2¼ cups toffee bits, divided

GANACHE

⅓ cup heavy cream

10 ounces semisweet chocolate, chopped

tip If you want perfectly level bars, use a sharp knife to level off the top near the edges, which tend to bake higher than the middle.

Preheat oven to 350°F. Line a 9-by-13-inch pan with parchment, leaving extra on two sides to later use as handles to remove the bars. Spray any portion of pan that isn't covered with parchment with nonstick spray.

Spread almonds in a single layer on a baking sheet. Toast almonds in oven for 7 minutes. Allow to cool on the pan. When almonds are cool enough to handle, chop coarsely.

In a mixing bowl, beat butter, sugars, and vanilla with a mixer for 3 to 4 minutes, until light and fluffy.

In a small mixing bowl, combine flour, baking powder, and salt. Add to the butter mixture and beat just until combined. Add ½ cup of the chopped almonds and 2 cups of the toffee bits to the mixture. Retain extras for topping.

Pour dough into the prepared pan and bake for 23 to 28 minutes, or until top is golden and a cake tester inserted comes out clean. Allow bars to cool.

To make the ganache: Heat 2 inches of water in the bottom of a double boiler. Heat heavy cream in the top of a double boiler until steaming hot but not boiling. Add the chocolate and stir until completely melted. Pour over bars and evenly spread across the top. Sprinkle extra chopped almonds and toffee bits on top of the ganache. Allow ganache to set completely.

Using a butter knife, loosen bars in any areas not covered with parchment. Lift bars out using parchment handles. Place on a cutting board and cut into 24 pieces. Store in an airtight container for up to 1 week.

PREHEAT **350°F** · BAKE TIME: 23–28 MINUTES · *MAKES* **24**

Mint is a traditional favorite at Christmastime, and nothing goes better with mint than chocolate. These rich treats are amazing and will add a festive green to your holiday spread. —J.K.

BROWNIES

8 ounces semisweet chocolate chips

½ cup unsalted butter, softened

2 eggs

½ cup brown sugar

¼ cup sugar

1 tablespoon vanilla extract

¼ cup unsweetened cocoa

¼ teaspoon salt

⅓ cup flour

MINT BUTTERCREAM

½ cup unsalted butter, softened

2 ounces cream cheese

2 tablespoons créme de menthe

1 teaspoon mint flavoring

2 cups confectioners' sugar

GANACHE

¾ cup semisweet chocolate chips

6 tablespoons heavy cream

Line an 8-by-8-inch pan with parchment, leaving extra on two sides to use as handles to later remove bars. Preheat oven to 350°F.

To make the brownies: In a heatproof bowl, melt chocolate chips in the microwave on low. Check and stir often. Be careful to heat only until the chips are melted. The chocolate should not be hot, but if it is, allow to cool before proceeding.

With a mixer, beat butter, eggs, sugars, and vanilla until fluffy, about 3 minutes. Add melted chocolate and beat until combined. Sift together cocoa, salt, and flour and add to the egg mixture. Beat on low until combined. Pour into prepared pan.

Bake for 18 to 22 minutes or until cake tester comes out clean. Set on rack and let cool completely.

To make buttercream: Beat butter and cream cheese with a mixer for about 3 minutes. Add the créme de menthe and mint flavoring. Slowly add confectioners' sugar and beat until combined.

Spread buttercream on the cooled brownies. Put in refrigerator until cold and firm.

To make the ganache: Place the chocolate chips in a heatproof bowl. Pour the cream in a small saucepan and heat just to boiling. Pour over chocolate chips and stir until chips are melted. Spread on buttercream.

Chill until chocolate is set. Using a butter knife, loosen bars in any areas not covered with parchment. Lift bars out using parchment handles. Place on a cutting board and cut into 24 pieces. Store in an airtight container for up to 1 week.

PREHEAT **350°F** BAKE TIME: 18–22 MINUTES *MAKES* **24**

APPLE DREAM BARS

This apple variation is a twist on vintage dream bars—a real hit for fans of apple pie. —J.K.

CRUST
2 cups flour
¾ cup brown sugar
¾ cup unsalted butter

APPLE MIXTURE
1 teaspoon cinnamon
½ cup sugar
3 cups apples, peeled, cored, and sliced

TOPPING
3 eggs
1 cup brown sugar
2 tablespoons flour
½ teaspoon salt
½ cup sweetened shredded coconut

Preheat oven to 375°F. Spray a 9-by-13-inch pan with nonstick spray.

In a medium bowl, whisk together flour and brown sugar. Slice the butter into small pats and toss into the sugar-flour mixture. Cut the butter and flour mixture with a pastry blender until you have a fine crumb. This step can also be achieved with a food processor. Pat the crust into the prepared pan.

Mix cinnamon and sugar. Spread sliced apples on crust and sprinkle with cinnamon-sugar mixture. Bake for 30 minutes.

While baking, mix the topping. Beat eggs and brown sugar for 2 to 3 minutes. Add flour, salt, and coconut and mix until incorporated. When crust with apples has finished baking, spread topping over apples and return to oven for 20 additional minutes. Cut bars in pan and serve warm. Or allow to cool and store in an airtight container for up to 1 week.

PREHEAT **375°**F   BAKE TIME: 50 MINUTES   *MAKES* **24**

DATE BARS

I adore baked goods with dates. These sweet, delectable, crumbly bars are totally irresistible. —J.K.

CRUMB MIXTURE
1½ cups flour
1½ cups old-fashioned oats
½ teaspoon baking soda
½ teaspoon salt
1 cup brown sugar
¾ cup unsalted butter

FILLING
1 pound chopped dates
¾ cup sugar
¾ cup water

Preheat oven to 375°F. Line a 9-by-13-inch pan with parchment, leaving extra on two sides to later use as handles to remove the bars. Spray any portion of pan that isn't covered with parchment with nonstick spray.

In a medium bowl, mix flour, oats, baking soda, salt, and brown sugar. Slice cold butter into pats and add to flour mixture. Cut with a pastry blender until crumbly. Pat half of the crumb mixture into prepared pan.

In a medium saucepan over medium-high heat, cook dates, sugar, and water until thick. Stir constantly so it doesn't burn. Spread on crumb mixture in pan. Sprinkle remaining crumb mixture on top on dates.

Bake 25 minutes or until top is golden brown. Allow bars to cool in pan. Using a butter knife, loosen bars in any areas not covered with parchment. Lift bars out using parchment handles. Place on a cutting board and cut into 24 pieces. Store in an airtight container for up to 1 week.

PREHEAT **350°F**   BAKE TIME: 25 MINUTES   *MAKES* **24**

MAGIC BARS

This it-just-wouldn't-be-Christmas-without-them classic was my friend Allison's most essential recipe during our holiday baking adventures. They were a favorite at her office and mine.
—L.K.

½ cup unsalted butter, melted

1¼ cups graham cracker crumbs

1¾ cups bittersweet chocolate chips

1 (14-ounce) can sweetened condensed milk

½ cup chopped pecans

1 cup sweetened shredded coconut

Line a 9-by-13-inch pan with parchment, leaving extra on two sides to later use as handles to remove the bars. Preheat oven to 350°F.

Pour melted butter into prepared pan. Sprinkle graham cracker crumbs over melted butter. Even out the mixture across the bottom of the pan with a rubber spatula.

Top graham crackers with chocolate chips. Drizzle sweetened condensed milk evenly over chocolate chips. Sprinkle chopped pecans on top of milk. Top with coconut.

Bake for about 45 minutes or until coconut is lightly browned. Allow bars to cool completely in the pan before removing. The chocolate needs to cool and set to cleanly cut the bars. Once bars are cool, remove them using the parchment handles and place them on a cutting board. Cut with a chef's knife into 8 rows by 5 rows. Store in an airtight container for up to 1 week.

Optional Layers: If you want to customize your magic bars, try adding a ½ cup of these optional layers: chopped dried cranberries or cherries, butterscotch chips, milk chocolate chips, peanut butter chips, white chocolate chips, or toffee bits.

PREHEAT **350**°F   BAKE TIME: 45 MINUTES   *MAKES* **40**

A decadent combination of favorite flavors, these bars will be a top choice for those who love rich treats. Warm a bar and top with ice cream for a decadent dessert.

BARS

1 cup (8.8 ounces) creamy peanut butter

1 cup unsalted butter, softened

1 cup sugar

1½ cups light brown sugar

1 tablespoon vanilla extract

3 eggs, room temperature

2⅔ cups flour

1 teaspoon baking soda

1 teaspoon salt

1 cup old-fashioned oats

2 cups dark chocolate chips

1 cup milk chocolate chips

CARAMEL FILLING

1 (11-ounce) bag caramel bits

½ cup heavy cream

Preheat oven to 350°F. Line a 9-by-13-inch pan with parchment, leaving extra on two sides to later use as handles to remove the bars. Spray any portion of pan that isn't covered with parchment with nonstick spray.

In a mixing bowl, beat peanut butter, butter, sugars, and vanilla with a mixer for about 3 minutes, until light and fluffy. Add eggs and beat on medium-high until well combined.

In a small mixing bowl, combine flour, baking soda, and salt. Add to the butter mixture and beat just until combined. Scrape the sides and bottom of bowl to ensure proper mixing. Add oats and chocolate chips. Beat just until combined.

In a medium saucepan, over medium heat, melt caramel with heavy cream. Stir constantly until caramel bits are completely melted and incorporated with the cream.

Scoop half of dough into the prepared pan and pat into pan evenly. Pour caramel mixture over dough. Cover caramel with remaining dough by dropping small pieces on top, distributing evenly.

Bake for 35 to 40 minutes, or until top is brown. Allow bars to cool in pan. Using a butter knife, loosen bars in any areas not covered with parchment. Lift bars out using parchment handles. Place on a cutting board and cut into 24 pieces. Store in an airtight container for up to 1 week.

PREHEAT **350°F**   BAKE TIME: 35-40 MINUTES   *MAKES* **24**

MARSHMALLOW CRISPY BROWNIES

I used to make these for dessert when I cooked Fellowship Supper at our church when my kids were young. They are gooey goodness and were always a crowd-pleaser. —J.K.

1 cup unsalted butter, softened

2 cups sugar

1 teaspoon vanilla extract

4 eggs

½ cup unsweetened cocoa

1 cup flour

½ teaspoon salt

7 ounces marshmallow creme

6 ounces semisweet chocolate chips

6 ounces butterscotch chips

1 cup peanut butter

3 cups crispy rice cereal

Preheat oven to 350°F. Line a 9-by-13-inch pan with parchment, leaving extra on two sides to later use as handles to remove the bars.

Beat butter, sugar, and vanilla until fluffy, about 3 minutes. Add eggs and beat until combined.

Over a medium bowl, sift cocoa to remove clumps. Add flour and salt, and whisk to combine. Add to the butter mixture and beat until well combined.

Pour into prepared pan and bake for about 25 minutes or until a cake tester inserted into the top of brownies comes out clean.

Spread marshmallow creme on top of brownies while still warm.

In a heatproof bowl, melt chocolate and butterscotch chips in microwave at 50 percent power for 1 minute. Stir with a rubber spatula. Continue to heat in 15-second intervals until completely melted. Stir in peanut butter. Add crispy rice cereal and spread on top of marshmallow creme.

Allow to cool completely. Remove the bars using the parchment handles and place on a cutting board. Cut with a chef's knife into 8 rows by 5 rows. Store in an airtight container for up to 1 week.

PREHEAT **350°F**   BAKE TIME: 20–25 MINUTES   *MAKES* **24**

CHAPTER

4

CHRISTMAS IS THE SWEETEST TIME

of the year. In our family, we make candy only for the holidays. Like the
twinkling lights, ribbons, and garlands—these recipes come out once a year.
Homemade marshmallows, chocolate-covered buttercreams, truffles, fudge,
brittles, and toffee are a joy to give and to taste.

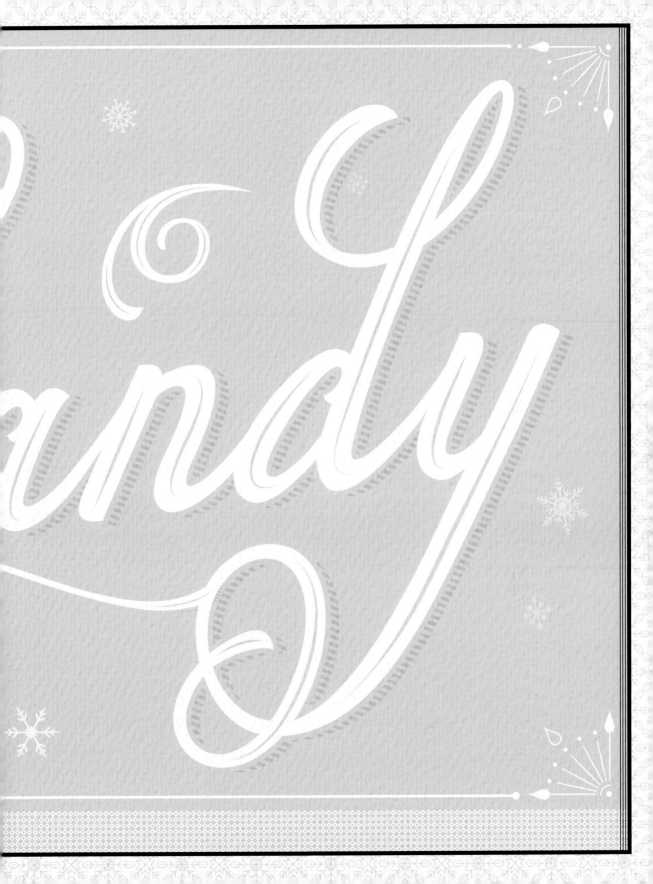

PEPPERMINT BARK

This easy wintry classic confection looks great on holiday trays and makes a fun gift.

12 ounces semisweet chocolate, coarsely chopped

1½ teaspoons peppermint extract

6 ounces white chocolate, coarsely chopped

½ cup coarsely chopped candy canes

Line a quarter-sheet rimmed pan or 9-by-13-inch pan with parchment and set aside.

In a double boiler, heat water to just a simmer in bottom pan. Water should not touch top pan. Place semisweet chocolate in top pan, taking care not to spill any water into the chocolate. Stir chocolate with a rubber spatula until melted. Add peppermint extract and stir until combined. Remove top pan and wipe away any water that may have condensed there with a towel. Pour into prepared pan and spread evenly.

Repeat melting process with white chocolate. Take care to ensure top pan is completely dry before adding chocolate. Pour melted white chocolate on top of semisweet chocolate and spread as evenly as possible. Marble the two chocolates with a butter knife. Evenly top chocolate with candy cane pieces.

Place tray in refrigerator for about 1 hour. Once the chocolate has set completely, remove from pan and break bark into chunks. Store in an airtight container for up to 2 weeks. Use parchment between layers to keep bark pieces from sticking to each other.

SERVES **20**

PRETZEL TOFFEE BARK

A twist on the salty-sweet goodness of chocolate-covered pretzels—this pretty bark is easy and delicious.

6 ounces semisweet chocolate, coarsely chopped

6 ounces milk chocolate, coarsely chopped

6 ounces white chocolate, coarsely chopped

1½ cups pretzels

½ cup toffee bits

Line a quarter-sheet rimmed pan or 9-by-13-inch pan with parchment and set aside.

In a double boiler, heat water to just a simmer in bottom pan. Water should not touch top pan. Place semisweet and milk chocolate in top pan, taking care to not spill any water into the chocolate. Stir chocolate with a rubber spatula until melted. Remove top pan and wipe away any water that may have condensed there with a towel. Pour into prepared pan and spread evenly.

Repeat melting process with white chocolate. Take care to ensure top pan is completely dry before adding chocolate. Pour melted white chocolate on top of semisweet chocolate and spread as evenly as possible. Marble the two chocolates with a butter knife. Evenly top chocolate with pretzels, pressing lightly on each pretzel so it is at least halfway pressed into chocolate. Sprinkle toffee bits over chocolate.

Place tray in refrigerator for about 1 hour. Once the chocolate has set completely, remove from pan and break bark into chunks. Store in an airtight container for up to 2 weeks.

SERVES **20**

My longtime friend Mary shared this recipe with me. She's been making them every Christmas for more than twenty-five years. The clusters have a maple buttercream center with a peanut and chocolate coating and remind me of a candy that was popular in the 1950s and '60s when I was a kid. —J.K.

½ cup unsalted butter, softened

4 ounces cream cheese

6 cups confectioners' sugar

8 teaspoons maple flavoring

5 pounds chocolate candy melts

2 pounds honey roasted peanuts

Line 2 large cookie sheets with parchment and set aside.

In a medium bowl, mix softened butter and cream cheese with a hand mixer. Add confectioners' sugar alternating with maple flavoring. When you're down to the last cup of confectioners' sugar, turn the buttercream out onto the counter and knead in the sugar by hand.

Melt chocolate in a small slow cooker set on warm.

Scoop 2 teaspoons maple cream, roll into a ball, flatten slightly into a disk, and place on one of the prepared cookie sheets. Continue placing disks of buttercream on the cookie sheet, leaving 4 inches between each. Cover each disk of maple cream with melted chocolate.

Place cookie sheets in refrigerator until chocolate sets. Remove from refrigerator and flip each buttercream so the chocolate side is down. Add about ¾ cup of the peanuts to the melted chocolate. Spoon chocolate with some peanuts to cover each maple cream. Add more peanuts as needed. It is best to add peanuts in batches because if they are in the warm chocolate too long, the honey coating can come off.

After all buttercreams are covered, allow chocolate to dry completely. Store in an airtight container in refrigerator for up to 2 weeks.

MAKES **50** CLUSTERS

Make your own box of chocolates with a variety of buttercreams. Use shapes, sprinkles, or chocolate drizzles to differentiate between the flavors. Customize the flavors with dark, milk, or white chocolate coatings.

VANILLA BEAN BUTTERCREAMS

¼ cup unsalted butter, softened

2¼ cups confectioners' sugar

1 tablespoon heavy cream

1 tablespoon vanilla bean paste

10 ounces bittersweet chocolate

White sprinkles, optional

LEMON BUTTERCREAMS

¼ cup unsalted butter, softened

2½ cups confectioners' sugar

2 tablespoons lemon juice

½ teaspoon fresh lemon zest

10 ounces white chocolate

Yellow sprinkles, optional

RASPBERRY BUTTERCREAMS

¼ cup unsalted butter, softened

2¼ cups confectioners' sugar

2 tablespoons Raspberry Jam
(see page 230)

½ teaspoon vanilla extract

10 ounces bittersweet chocolate

(Ingredients continued)

Line a baking sheet with parchment and set aside. In a medium bowl, beat butter and confectioners' sugar for 2 minutes. Add remaining ingredients and beat until completely incorporated. Use a 2-teaspoon ice cream scoop for small buttercreams or a 1-tablespoon scoop for large buttercreams. Scoop onto prepared baking sheet. Leave buttercreams in the shape of the scoop or flatten into a disk. Alternately form squares or logs. See tip below.

If using sprinkles or crushed candy to decorate, set out near work area. Melt chocolate in a double boiler or microwave. Dip each buttercream in chocolate and return to lined baking sheet. If topping with sprinkles or candy, do so immediately before chocolate has a chance to set. Allow chocolate to set completely. Drizzle with extra chocolate if desired.

After chocolate has set completely, store in an airtight container in refrigerator for up to 3 weeks or out of refrigerator for 4 to 5 days. Buttercreams taste best at room temperature, so remove from refrigerator about an hour before serving.

tip

If you're making more than one flavor, mold each flavor into a different shape or top with different-colored sprinkles to easily see which is which. Include a little guide to flavors when gifting a variety of buttercreams.

MAPLE PECAN BUTTERCREAMS

¼ cup unsalted butter, softened

2½ cups confectioners' sugar

2 tablespoons pure maple syrup

2 tablespoons chopped pecans

10 ounces milk chocolate

CHOCOLATE BUTTERCREAMS

¼ cup unsalted butter, softened

2¼ cups confectioners' sugar

2 tablespoons unsweetened cocoa

1 tablespoon heavy cream

1 teaspoon vanilla extract

10 ounces milk chocolate

PEPPERMINT MOCHA BUTTERCREAMS

¼ cup unsalted butter, softened

2¼ cups confectioners' sugar

2 tablespoons unsweetened cocoa

1 teaspoon espresso powder

1 tablespoon heavy cream

1 teaspoon peppermint extract

10 ounces bittersweet chocolate

Crushed peppermint candy, optional

MAKES **28** SMALL BUTTERCREAMS OF EACH FLAVOR

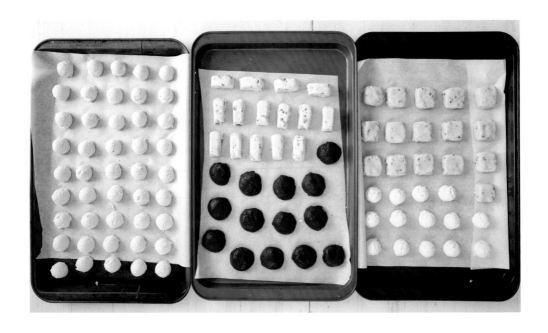

PEANUT BUTTER TRUFFLE SQUARES

These confections are inspired by the popular Christmas staples known as buckeyes and peanut butter balls. This variation is rich with a pleasant candy crunch from the red and green mini M&M's. —L.K.

4 ounces cream cheese

¾ cup unsalted butter, softened

1½ cups (13.2 ounces) creamy peanut butter

¾ cup brown sugar

4 cups confectioners' sugar

1 cup Christmas Mini M&M's

15–20 ounces semisweet chocolate, roughly chopped

1½ ounces milk chocolate, roughly chopped, for drizzle

Line a 9-by-13-inch pan with parchment, leaving extra on two sides to later use as handles.

Beat together cream cheese, butter, peanut butter, and brown sugar until well combined. Add confectioners' sugar 1 cup at a time. Mix in Christmas Mini M&M's. Press peanut butter mixture into prepared pan. Refrigerate mixture in pan for about 1 hour, up to overnight.

Remove cold peanut butter slab from pan using the parchment handles. Place on a cutting board and make 8 cuts to make 9 rows along the long side and 5 cuts to make 6 rows along the short side, to create 54 pieces, roughly 1⅓-inch squares. Place squares on two parchment-lined cookie sheets. For rounded corners on your final truffle, push in the top four corners slightly.

In a double boiler, heat water to just a simmer in bottom pan. Water should not touch top pan. Place chocolate in top pan. Stir chocolate with a rubber spatula until melted.

Dip squares in melted chocolate, allowing excess chocolate to drip off before placing back on parchment. If during the process your chocolate starts to thicken, return pan to the double boiler and warm it back up just until the chocolate is workable.

After chocolate has set, melt milk chocolate, if using. With a fork, drizzle milk chocolate over squares with a fast diagonal motion. Allow milk chocolate to set and then store in an airtight container in the refrigerator for up to 2 weeks.

MAKES **54** SQUARES

Decadent and richly chocolatey, these are especially for extra-dark chocolate lovers. If you want a little more sweetness, replace the bittersweet chocolate with semisweet chocolate.

TRUFFLE

10 ounces bittersweet chocolate, finely chopped

¾ cup heavy cream

2 tablespoons unsalted butter

1 tablespoon vanilla extract

COATING

½ cup Dutch process or unsweetened cocoa

Place chocolate in a medium heatproof bowl.

Heat heavy cream, butter, and vanilla in a saucepan over medium-high heat until it is steaming hot and just about to boil. Pour over chocolate. Stir with a rubber spatula until chocolate is completely melted and incorporated. If chocolate doesn't melt completely, set bowl with chocolate over a pan with simmering water. Stir until chocolate is completely melted.

Cover bowl with plastic wrap and refrigerate for 2 hours or overnight. Once mixture has chilled, line baking tray with parchment. Place cocoa in a small bowl. Using a 2-teaspoon cookie scoop, scoop and roll into a ball by hand. Roll truffle in cocoa, coating it completely. Place on prepared baking tray. Continue with the remaining chocolate mixture. Store in an airtight container in the refrigerator for up to 2 weeks. Remove from refrigerator about an hour before serving.

MAKES **45** TRUFFLES

tip | For 2 tones of truffles, roll half in Dutch process cocoa and half in unsweetened cocoa.

MALTED MILK
CHOCOLATE TRUFFLES

These sweet truffles are great for milk chocolate lovers and are reminiscent of a malted milkshake.

TRUFFLE

7 ounces milk chocolate, finely chopped

3 ounces semisweet chocolate, finely chopped

¾ cup heavy cream

⅓ cup malted milk powder

1 tablespoons unsalted butter

1 teaspoon vanilla extract

COATING

¼ cup Dutch process or unsweetened cocoa

¼ cup malted milk powder

Place chocolate in a medium heatproof bowl.

Heat heavy cream, malted milk powder, butter, and vanilla extract in a saucepan over medium-high heat until it is steaming hot and just about to boil. Pour over chocolate. Stir with a rubber spatula until chocolate is completely melted and incorporated. If chocolate doesn't melt completely, set bowl with chocolate over a pan with simmering water. Stir until chocolate is completely melted.

Cover bowl with plastic wrap and refrigerate for 2 hours or overnight. Once mixture has chilled, line baking tray with parchment. Whisk together cocoa and malted milk powder in a small bowl. Using a 2-teaspoon cookie scoop, scoop and roll into a ball by hand. Roll truffle in cocoa, coating it completely. Place on prepared baking tray. Continue with the remaining chocolate mixture. Store in an airtight container in the refrigerator for up to 2 weeks. Remove from refrigerator about an hour before serving.

MAKES **45** TRUFFLES

tip For 2 tones of truffles, add 2 tablespoons confectioners' sugar to the coating halfway through the process.

SEA FOAM CANDY

My friend Yvonne shared this recipe with me years ago. They are melt-in-your-mouth delicious and are great for sharing. —J.K.

1 cup sugar

1 cup dark corn syrup

1 tablespoon white vinegar

1 tablespoon baking soda

1 pound semisweet chocolate, coarsely chopped

1 teaspoon vegetable shortening

Butter a 9-by-9-inch pan. Set aside.

Clip a candy thermometer to a large saucepan. Combine sugar, corn syrup, and vinegar in pan. Cook over medium heat, stirring constantly, until sugar is dissolved. Bring to a boil and cook without stirring until the temperature reaches 300°F on candy thermometer.

Remove from heat and quickly stir in baking soda. Use caution; mixture will foam and bubble. Pour into prepared pan. Cool completely and break into pieces.

Line 2 cookie sheets with parchment and set aside.

In a double boiler, heat water to just a simmer in bottom pan. Water should not touch top pan. Place chocolate and shortening in top pan, taking care not to spill any water into the chocolate. Stir chocolate with a rubber spatula until melted. Remove top pan from double boiler and set on towel on counter.

Dip candy pieces in chocolate; allow excess chocolate to drip off before placing back on parchment. If during the process, your chocolate starts to thicken, return pan to the double boiler and warm it back up just until the chocolate is workable. Once the chocolate has set completely, store in an airtight container for up to 2 weeks. Use parchment between layers to keep candies from sticking to each other.

COOK TO **300°F**   *SERVES* **24**

ALMOND TOFFEE

Toffee is a Christmas tradition at our house and has always been part of my holiday care packages to friends and colleagues. —L.K.

⅓ cup whole almonds

1½ cups unsalted butter

1⅔ cups sugar

½ cup water

2 teaspoon salt

1 vanilla bean or 1 tablespoon vanilla bean paste

8 ounces semisweet chocolate

Preheat oven to 350°F. Line a half-sheet baking pan with parchment or a baking mat and set on a hot pad on the counter near your stove.

Spread almonds in a single layer on a small baking sheet. Toast almonds in oven for 7 minutes. Allow to cool on the pan. When almonds are cool enough to handle, chop coarsely.

Clip a candy thermometer to a large pot and set hot pads within reach of the stove. Mix butter, sugar, water, and salt in the saucepan and cook over medium heat. Cut vanilla bean lengthwise and scrape seeds out and add to mixture.

Boil at medium-high heat. Stir constantly until temperature reaches 300°F and toffee has turned golden. Using hot pads, remove from heat immediately and pour on prepared pan. Use caution; mixture is extremely hot. Spread by shaking pans from side to side.

Cool completely. With a paper towel, wipe any grease from the top of the toffee. Melt chocolate and spread over toffee. Sprinkle chopped almonds on melted chocolate. Allow chocolate to set completely.

Break into pieces and store in an airtight container for up to 2 weeks.

COOK TO **300°F**

SERVES **24**

CASHEW BRITTLE

Brittles have been a Christmas tradition at my house for more than forty years. Pick up some Christmas tins and package this up as gifts for family, friends, and teachers. —J.K.

2 cups sugar

1 cup light corn syrup

½ cup water

½ teaspoon salt

2 sticks unsalted butter + more for the cookie sheet

2 cups cashews

1 teaspoon baking soda

Butter 2 cookie sheets and set on hot pads.

Clip a candy thermometer to a large saucepan.

Mix sugar, corn syrup, water, and salt in the saucepan and cook over medium heat. When it starts to boil, add butter.

Boil at medium heat, stirring constantly. When the mixture reaches 280°F, add cashews.

Adding the cashews cools the mixture, and it takes a while for the temperature go back up. Stir constantly until temperature reaches 300°F.

Take off burner and add baking soda. Use caution; mixture will bubble up when you add the baking soda.

Mix well and pour onto the prepared cookie sheets. Spread by shaking pans from side to side. Some air bubbles should remain.

Cool completely.

Break into pieces and store in an airtight container for up to 2 weeks.

COOK TO **250°F**

SERVES **50**

VANILLA BEAN CHOCOLATE FUDGE

This has been my favorite candy to make for Christmas for years. When I make homemade holiday gifts for clients, individually wrapped fudge is always part of my care packages. —L.K.

2½ cups heavy cream

½ cup milk

½ cup light corn syrup

½ cup water

2 tablespoons unsalted butter

1¾ cups sugar

1¾ cups dark brown sugar

1 teaspoon salt

1 vanilla bean or 1 tablespoon vanilla bean paste

5 ounces bittersweet chocolate, coarsely chopped

Line a 9-by-13-inch pan with parchment, leaving a little extra on two sides to later use as handles to remove the fudge. Set near the stove on a hot pad. Place your coarsely chopped chocolate near your stove. When mixture reaches temperature, you won't have much time before the fudge starts to solidify, so getting everything in place in advance is helpful.

Clip a candy thermometer to a 7-quart or bigger pot or Dutch oven. While cooking, the mixture bubbles a lot, so a large pot is essential.

Add all ingredients to the pot except the vanilla bean and chocolate. Cut vanilla bean lengthwise. Scrape out the seeds and add them to the pot. Over medium heat, whisk ingredients until combined. Increase heat to medium-high and continue to stir.

Do not leave pot unattended. If mixture boils near the top of pot, reduce heat. Stir continuously until mixture reaches 250°F. Turn off heat and add chocolate. The heat from the fudge will melt the chocolate. Stir until combined. Work quickly—the fudge sets rapidly as it cools. Pour into prepared pan. Allow to set completely.

Remove the fudge with the parchment handles and place on a cutting board. Cut into small pieces and wrap individually in wax paper or parchment. Store individually wrapped fudge in an airtight container for up to 2 weeks.

COOK TO **250°**F

MAKES **50**

DIVINITY

This old-fashioned nougat-like candy was a family tradition when I was growing up. My Aunt Meme made divinity every Christmas. Back then, candy thermometers weren't as common as they are now. To test if the candy had reached the right temperature, my aunt would put a little of the cooked sugar in cold water to see how firm it was. —J.K.

2 cups sugar

½ cup light corn syrup

½ cup water

2 egg whites, room temperature

¼ teaspoon salt

1½ teaspoons vanilla extract

¾ cup chopped pecans

Place 2 to 3 feet of parchment on counter.

In a medium pot, cook sugar, corn syrup, and water over medium-high heat. Clip a candy thermometer to the side of the pot. Heat to 250°F.

While the mixture is cooking, prepare egg whites. In the bowl of a stand mixer with whisk attachment, beat egg whites and salt until peaks form.

When mixture on the stove reaches 250°F, take off stove and pour slowly into egg whites, beat at high speed.

Add vanilla and keep beating at high speed until it holds shape, about 6 minutes. Stir in pecans.

Coat 2 teaspoons with nonstick spray and scoop spoonfuls onto prepared parchment. Work quickly—the candy hardens quickly as it cools.

Allow divinity to dry a few hours. Store in airtight container.

COOK TO **250°F**   SERVES **50**

SUGARED PECANS

These festive pecans are great for snacking and are perfect for parties or packaged in a mason jar with a ribbon as a gift. —J.K.

Butter for cookie sheet
1 egg white
1 tablespoon cold water
1 cup sugar
1 teaspoon cinnamon
1 teaspoon salt
1 pound whole pecan halves

Preheat oven to 250°F. Butter a cookie sheet and set aside.

In a large bowl, whip egg white and water until peaks form.

In a small bowl, combine sugar, cinnamon, and salt and add to egg white. Add pecans and mix thoroughly. Spread on buttered cookie sheet and bake 1 hour, stirring every 15 minutes. Cool and store in airtight container for up to 2 weeks.

PREHEAT **250°F**   BAKE TIME: 1 HOUR   *MAKES* **4** CUPS

Once you've tried a homemade marshmallow, the ones from the store will no longer be good enough. They are extra soft and make a decadent top to hot chocolate. Package in a cellophane bag with a ribbon for a feel-good, cozy gift.

1½ cups water, divided

4 envelopes unflavored gelatin

3 cups sugar

¾ cup corn syrup

½ teaspoon salt

2 tablespoons vanilla bean paste

2 cups confectioners' sugar, plus more for the pan

Generously spray a 9-by-13-inch pan with nonstick spray. Coat the pan with confectioners' sugar and set aside.

In the bowl of a stand mixer, combine ½ cup water and gelatin. Use whisk attachment. Mix for 10 seconds and allow to bloom.

Clip a candy thermometer to a large pot and set hot pads within reach of the stove. Cook 1 cup water, sugar, corn syrup, salt, and vanilla bean paste over medium-high heat. Stir constantly until mixture reaches 240°F. Use hot pads to remove pot from stove and pour into mixer bowl over gelatin. Start mixer on lowest setting and gradually increase the speed to high. Mix for 10 to 12 minutes, stopping occasionally to scrape down the bowl. Mixture will be fluffy and very sticky.

Pour marshmallow mixture into prepared pan. Allow to cool and then cover pan with plastic wrap. Allow marshmallows to set for at least 4 hours.

Place confectioners' sugar in a bowl. Generously dust a cutting board with some of the sugar. Turn out marshmallows on cutting board. Sprinkle more confectioners' sugar on the slab of marshmallows. Cut 8 rows on the long side and 6 rows on the short side. Add more confectioners' sugar if the knife gets too sticky. Coat each cut marshmallow in confectioners' sugar to keep them from sticking to each other.

Store in an airtight container for up to 2 weeks.

COOK TO **240°F**

MAKES **50**

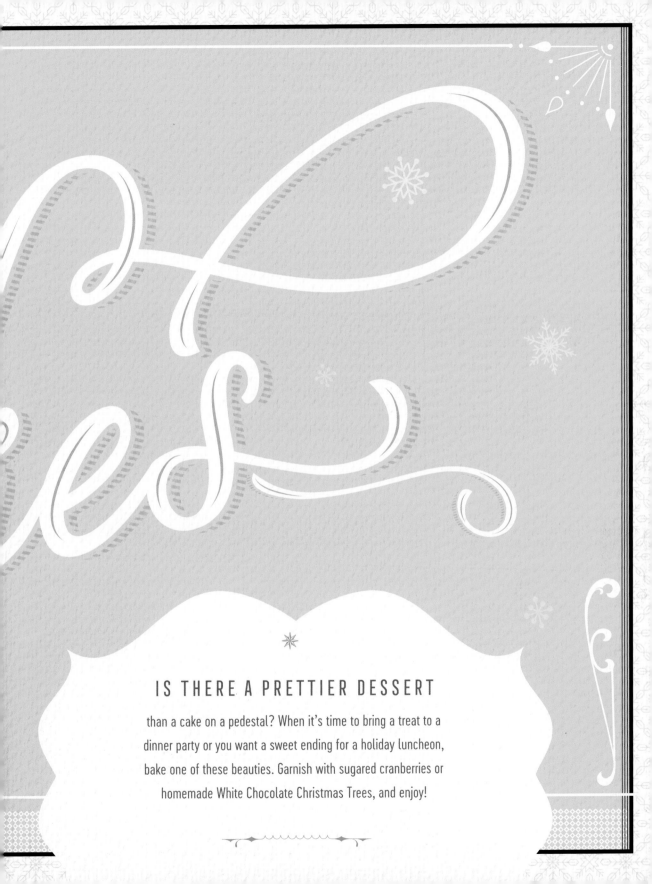

IS THERE A PRETTIER DESSERT

than a cake on a pedestal? When it's time to bring a treat to a
dinner party or you want a sweet ending for a holiday luncheon,
bake one of these beauties. Garnish with sugared cranberries or
homemade White Chocolate Christmas Trees, and enjoy!

I made this cake for our church dessert auction and it was a big hit. A bright red cake topped with cream cheese frosting and colorful trees makes the perfect Christmas cake—with rich flavors it tastes even better than it looks. —J.K.

1 cup unsalted butter, softened

2 cups granulated sugar

½ cup canola or vegetable oil

4 large eggs, room temperature

1 tablespoon vanilla extract

3 cups cake flour

1½ teaspoons baking soda

3 tablespoons unsweetened cocoa powder

1 teaspoon salt

1½ teaspoons apple cider vinegar

4 tablespoons gel red food coloring

1 cup buttermilk

¼ cup Simple Syrup (see page 248), optional

Cream Cheese Frosting (see page 240)

White Chocolate Christmas Trees, optional (see page 244)

Spray two 9-inch cake pans generously with nonstick spray and set aside. Preheat oven to 350°F.

In a stand mixer with the paddle attachment, beat butter, sugar, and oil on medium-high speed until well combined, about 3 minutes. Add eggs and vanilla and beat on medium-high for 3 minutes.

In a medium bowl, combine the flour, baking soda, cocoa powder, and salt. Add to butter mixture and beat on low until combined. Add vinegar, food coloring, and buttermilk and beat on low until combined. Scrape the bowl, including the bottom, to ensure all ingredients are evenly combined.

Pour into prepared pans.

Bake for 25 to 35 minutes or until cake tester comes out clean. Set on rack and let cool for 10 minutes before turning out the layers onto parchment. When cakes are cool enough to handle, turn them over and level the tops with a bread knife. Allow cakes to cool completely before frosting.

Spread a small dab of frosting to a serving plate or cake stand and place the first layer cut-side down on the plate. If using simple syrup, apply to the first layer with a pastry brush, and allow it to soak into the cake for about 2 minutes. With an offset spatula, frost the first layer with cream cheese frosting. Repeat for second layer.

Serve the same day. To save uneaten cake, slice and store in an airtight container to keep up to 4 days or freeze for up to 3 months.

PREHEAT **350°F** · BAKE TIME: 25–35 MINUTES · *SERVES* **18**

MAPLE LAYER CAKE WITH RASPBERRY BUTTERCREAM

I love using maple as a natural alternative to sugar. This buttery layer cake has a mild maple flavor and pairs beautifully with the raspberry buttercream. —L.K.

1½ cups unsalted butter

1½ cups pure maple syrup, room temperature

4 eggs, room temperature

1 tablespoon vanilla extract

3¾ cups cake flour, divided

2 teaspoons baking powder

½ teaspoon baking soda

1 teaspoon salt

1¼ cups buttermilk

¼ cup pure maple syrup, optional

Raspberry Buttercream (see page 238)

Spray three 8-inch cake pans generously with nonstick spray and set aside. Preheat oven to 350°F.

In a stand mixer with the paddle attachment, beat butter and maple syrup on medium-high speed until well combined, about 4 minutes. Add eggs, vanilla, and 1 cup of the flour, and beat on medium-high for 2 to 3 minutes.

In a medium bowl, combine the remaining flour, baking powder, baking soda, and salt. Add to butter mixture and beat on low until combined. Add buttermilk and beat on low until combined. Scrape the bowl, including the bottom, to ensure all ingredients are evenly combined. Pour into prepared pans.

Bake for 25 to 35 minutes or until cake tester comes out clean. Set on rack and let cool for 10 minutes before turning out the layers onto parchment. When cakes are cool enough to handle, turn them over and level the tops with a bread knife. Allow cakes to cool completely before frosting.

Spread a small dab of frosting on a serving plate or cake stand and place the first layer, cut-side down, on the plate. With a pastry brush, apply maple syrup to the first layer. Allow it to soak into the cake for about 2 minutes. With an offset spatula, frost the first layer with raspberry buttercream. Repeat with all three layers.

Serve the same day. To save uneaten cake, slice and store in an airtight container. Keep up to 4 days or freeze for up to 3 months.

PREHEAT **350°F**   BAKE TIME: 25–35 MINUTES   *SERVES* **18**

CHOCOLATE CAKE WITH PEPPERMINT FILLING

Rich and fudgy this chocolate layer cake pairs nicely with peppermint buttercream filling. Pipe filling in rings of red and white for a candy stripe center. —L.K.

CAKE

½ cup unsalted butter, softened

1¾ cups granulated sugar

½ cup canola or vegetable oil

4 large eggs, room temperature

1 tablespoon vanilla extract

¾ cup unsweetened cocoa powder

3 cups cake flour

1½ teaspoons baking soda

1½ teaspoons baking powder

1 teaspoon salt

¾ cup buttermilk

½ cup hot coffee

Chocolate Buttercream (see page 239)

¼ cup Simple Syrup (see page 248), optional

PEPPERMINT FILLING

¾ teaspoon peppermint extract

Half batch Vanilla Buttercream (see page 237)

Spray two 9-inch cake pans generously with nonstick spray and set aside. Preheat oven to 350°F.

In a stand mixer with the paddle attachment, beat butter, sugar, and oil on medium-high speed until well combined, about 3 minutes. Add eggs and vanilla and beat on medium-high for 2 to 3 minutes.

Sift cocoa into a medium bowl. Add flour, baking soda, baking powder, and salt and stir to combine. Add to butter mixture and beat on low until combined. Add buttermilk and beat on low until combined. Add hot coffee and beat for one minute. Scrape the bowl, including the bottom, to ensure all ingredients are evenly combined. Pour into prepared pans.

Bake for 30 to 40 minutes or until cake tester comes out clean. Set on rack and let cool for 10 minutes before turning out the layers onto parchment. When cakes are cool enough to handle, turn them over and level the tops with a bread knife. Allow cakes to cool completely before frosting.

Spread a small dab of frosting to a serving plate or cake stand and place the first layer cut-side down on the plate. If using simple syrup, apply to the first layer with a pastry brush, and allow it to soak into the cake for about 2 minutes.

Add peppermint extract to Vanilla Buttercream. See next page for how to pipe filling. Frost exterior of cake with Chocolate Buttercream. Serve the same day. To save uneaten cake, slice and store in an airtight container. Keep up to 4 days.

PREHEAT **350°F** · BAKE TIME: 30–40 MINUTES · *SERVES* **36**

Color half of the peppermint buttercream red and place in piping bag. Put remaining half in a piping bag and about 1 cup chocolate buttercream in a third piping bag.

Pipe a thick ring of chocolate buttercream around bottom layer of cake.

Pipe a thick red ring within the chocolate ring.

Pipe a white ring within the red and repeat, alternating red and white until you reach the center.

Top with second chocolate cake layer. Use the chocolate piping bag to fill in gaps between the two layers. Frost cake and top with crushed peppermint candies.

A seriously delicious wintry treat, these cupcakes taste great while sipping coffee fireside on a snowy day.

6 tablespoons unsalted butter

¾ cup vegetable oil

2 cups sugar

4 egg whites + 1 egg

1½ teaspoon vanilla extract

¾ cup coconut milk

2⅔ cups cake flour

1 tablespoon baking powder

½ teaspoon baking soda

1 teaspoon salt

1½ cups sweetened shredded coconut, divided

½ batch Cream Cheese Frosting (see page 240)

Line two 12-cup muffin pans with white cupcake liners. Preheat oven to 350°F.

In a stand mixer with the paddle attachment, beat butter, oil, and sugar on medium-high speed until well combined, about 4 minutes. Add eggs, vanilla, and coconut milk, and beat on medium-high for 3 minutes.

In a medium bowl, combine flour, baking powder, baking soda, and salt. Add to butter mixture and beat on low until combined. Add ½ cup shredded coconut and beat on low until combined. Scrape the bowl, including the bottom, to ensure all ingredients are evenly combined. Scoop into prepared muffin pans.

Bake for 18 to 20 minutes or until cake tester comes out clean. Set on rack and let cool for 5 minutes before removing cupcakes from pan. Allow cupcakes to cool completely before frosting.

With an offset spatula, frost each cupcake with Cream Cheese Frosting and sprinkle with remaining coconut.

Store in an airtight container for up to 4 days or freeze for up to 3 months.

PREHEAT **350°F**   BAKE TIME: 18-20 MINUTES   *MAKES* **24**

GINGERBREAD BUNDT CAKE

The rich, spicy smell of gingerbread in the oven is quintessential Christmas. This cake is a joy to bake and, when placed on a pedestal cake stand, is a gorgeous dessert to bring to a holiday gathering.

1 cup unsalted butter, softened

1 cup dark brown sugar

⅓ cup pure maple syrup, room temperature

⅓ cup unsulfured molasses

4 eggs, room temperature

1 tablespoon vanilla extract

2¾ cups flour

1 teaspoon baking powder

1 teaspoon baking soda

½ teaspoon salt

4 teaspoons Gingerbread Spice (see page 247) or 1½ teaspoons ground ginger, 1½ teaspoons cinnamon, ½ teaspoon ground cloves, and ½ teaspoon allspice

1 cup buttermilk

Vanilla Bean Glaze (see page 234)

Fresh rosemary for garnish, optional

Fresh pomegranate seeds for garnish, optional

Spray a 12-cup Bundt pan with nonstick spray and set aside. Preheat oven to 350°F.

In a stand mixer with the paddle attachment, beat butter, brown sugar, maple syrup, and molasses on medium-high speed until well combined and fluffy, about 4 minutes. Scrape the bowl, including the bottom, to ensure all ingredients are evenly combined. Add eggs and vanilla and beat for 1 more minute.

In a medium bowl, combine flour, baking powder, baking soda, salt, and gingerbread spice. Add to butter mixture and beat on low until combined. Add buttermilk and beat on low until combined. Once again, scrape the bowl, including the bottom, to ensure all ingredients are evenly combined.

Pour into prepared pan.

Bake for 30 to 35 minutes or until a cake tester comes out clean. Set on rack and let cool for 10 minutes before turning it out on a serving plate or cake stand.

Allow to cool completely and then drizzle glaze and add garnishes, if using. Serve the same day. To save uneaten cake, slice and store in an airtight container for up to 4 days.

tip   If your Bundt pan is smaller than 12 cups, be careful not to overfill. Your pan should be no more than three quarters full with batter. If your pan is too small, bake extra batter in a muffin pan.

PREHEAT **350°**F   ✳ BAKE TIME: 30–35 MINUTES ✳   *SERVES* **16**

CLEMENTINE CRANBERRY
BUNDT CAKE

December is a great month to find fresh cranberries in produce departments. Enjoy those tart little treats in this moist Bundt cake. Garnish with sugared cranberries and serve on a pedestal for a merry presentation.

10 tablespoons (1 stick + 2 tablespoons) unsalted butter, softened

4 ounces cream cheese

1½ cups sugar

3 eggs, room temperature

1 teaspoon vanilla extract

Zest of 1 clementine

1 tablespoon clementine juice

2 cups flour

1 teaspoon baking powder

½ teaspoon salt

½ cup heavy cream

1½ cups fresh cranberries

Maple Glaze (see page 234)

Sugared Cranberries, for garnish (see page 229), optional

Spray a 12-cup Bundt pan with nonstick spray and set aside. Preheat oven to 350°F.

In a stand mixer with the paddle attachment, beat butter, cream cheese, and sugar on medium-high speed until fluffy, about 3 minutes. Scrape the bowl, including the bottom, to ensure all ingredients are evenly combined. Add eggs, vanilla, and clementine zest and juice, and beat for 1 more minute on high.

In a medium bowl, combine flour, baking powder, and salt. Add to butter mixture and beat on low until combined. Add heavy cream and beat on low until combined. Scrape the bowl, including the bottom, to ensure all ingredients are evenly combined.

With a rubber spatula, stir in cranberries. Pour into prepared pan.

Bake for 40 to 50 minutes or until a cake tester comes out clean. Set on rack and let cool for 10 minutes before turning it out on a serving plate or cake stand.

Allow to cool completely and then drizzle glaze and add garnishes, if using. Serve the same day. To save uneaten cake, slice and store in an airtight container for up to 4 days or freeze for up to 3 months.

PREHEAT **350°F**   BAKE TIME: 40–50 MINUTES   *SERVES* **16**

KIWI RASPBERRY CHRISTMAS CAKE

With red and green fruit, this cake is perfect for celebrating Christmas. I brought this to our family's Christmas Day brunch last year and it was a hit. It also makes a nice dessert for an evening party. Garnish with fruit for flare and extra-fresh flavor. —J.K.

¾ cup unsalted butter

1 cup sugar

3 eggs, room temperature

1 teaspoon vanilla extract

1¾ cups flour

2 teaspoons baking powder

½ teaspoon salt

⅔ cup buttermilk

2 kiwis, diced, plus more for garnish

1 cup raspberries, plus more for garnish

Vanilla Bean Whipped Cream (see page 240)

Raspberry Compote (see page 191)

Spray a 10-inch or 11-inch cake pan with nonstick spray and set aside. Preheat oven to 350°F.

In a stand mixer with the paddle attachment, beat butter and sugar on medium-high speed until well combined and fluffy, about 3 minutes. Scrape the bowl, including the bottom, to ensure all ingredients are evenly combined. Add eggs and vanilla and beat for 1 more minute on high speed.

In a medium bowl, combine flour, baking powder, and salt. Add to butter mixture and beat on low until combined. Add buttermilk, and beat on low until combined. Scrape the bowl, including the bottom, to ensure all ingredients are evenly combined.

With a rubber spatula, stir in kiwi, and raspberries. Pour into prepared pan.

Bake for 30 to 40 minutes or until cake tester comes out clean. Set on rack and let cool for 10 minutes before turning it out on a serving plate or cake stand.

Allow to cool completely. When ready to serve, top center of cake with whipped cream. Drizzle with raspberry compote and garnish with extra fruit. Serve immediately. To save uneaten cake, slice and store in an airtight container in the refrigerator for up to 3 days.

PREHEAT **350°F**　　　BAKE TIME: 30–40 MINUTES　　　*SERVES* **16**

Cheesecake is always a hit, and I love to bring this mint and chocolate version to Christmas gatherings. Cheesecake is best if refrigerated overnight, so remember to make it a day ahead of your party. —J.K.

CRUST

2½ cups Oreo cookie crumbs

¼ cup melted unsalted butter

FILLING

4 (8-ounce) packages cream cheese, softened

1 cup sugar

1 cup sour cream

½ teaspoon peppermint extract

⅓ cup crème de menthe syrup

4 eggs

1½ cups mini chocolate chips

GANACHE

⅔ cup heavy cream

5 ounces semisweet chocolate, coarsely chopped

OPTIONAL GARNISH

½ cup chocolate pearls

Preheat oven to 350°F. Spray a 10-inch springform pan with nonstick spray.

For the crust, mix Oreo cookie crumbs and melted butter. Spread on bottom and partially up the side of the prepared pan.

Beat cream cheese and sugar. Add sour cream, peppermint extract, and crème de menthe. Beat until smooth and then beat in eggs. Scrape the bowl, including the bottom, to ensure all ingredients are evenly combined. Stir in mini chocolate chips. Pour over crust.

Bake for 50 minutes or until center is about set. Run a knife around the edge of pan to loosen. Cool in pan on wire rack.

For the ganache, heat heavy cream in a medium saucepan over medium-high heat until steaming hot but not boiling. Remove from heat and add chocolate. Stir continuously until chocolate is smooth. Pour over cheesecake. Allow to cool completely. Cover pan with plastic wrap and refrigerate overnight.

Carefully remove side of pan and serve. Store uneaten cheesecake in the refrigerator for up to a week.

PREHEAT **350°F**   BAKE TIME: 50 MINUTES   *SERVES* **15**

rning e

WITH PRESENTS WRAPPED IN PRETTY PAPER

tied with ribbons stacked under the tree, and the smell of fresh coffee brewing,

the kids filled with excitement and wonder—Christmas morning is a joy.

Whether you are entertaining out-of-town guests or cooking up a celebratory

breakfast for your family, these dishes will brighten your morning.

Star bread takes a little bit of time to prepare, but will make your Christmas morning extra special and fill your home with amazing smells. —L.K.

YEAST MIXTURE
1 cup whole milk, warm

2¼ teaspoons yeast

1 teaspoon sugar

DOUGH MIXTURE
⅓ cup unsalted butter, melted

⅓ cup sugar

¼ cup buttermilk, warm

1 egg

1 teaspoon vanilla extract

3½–4 cups flour

1 teaspoon salt

CINNAMON MIXTURE
2 teaspoons cinnamon

½ cup sugar

¼ cup unsalted butter, softened

EGG WASH
1 egg, beaten

OPTIONAL TOPPINGS
Confectioners' sugar

Maple Glaze (see page 234)

In a small bowl, whisk together yeast mixture ingredients. Allow to set until foamy, about 10 minutes.

In a stand mixer with the paddle attachment, combine the first 5 dough ingredients. Pour in the yeast mixture. Stir the salt into 2 cups of the flour and add it to the dough mixture and beat until combined.

Switch to the dough hook and add remaining flour ½ cup at a time. Add flour until a soft, shaggy dough forms. Beat dough for 4 minutes. The dough should easily stick together in a ball and still be a little sticky.

Remove the dough hook and loosely cover the dough with plastic wrap. Allow dough to rise in a warm place for 1 hour.

Line a half-sheet baking pan with parchment. Mix cinnamon and sugar and set aside.

On a lightly floured work surface, evenly divide the dough into 4 equal pieces and form balls with each piece. Using a floured rolling pin, roll out the first ball in as round a shape as possible. The finished piece should measure about 10 inches across. Trim the edges to create a circle. Transfer the first round to the prepared baking pan. To avoid stretching the dough, you can wrap it around the rolling pin to help move it.

Spread ⅓ of the softened butter evenly on the first layer of dough and sprinkle with ⅓ of the cinnamon mixture.

(continued)

Roll out the remaining rounds, adding butter and cinnamon mixture on layers 2 and 3. Do not add anything on top of the fourth layer.

Mark the center of the dough with a 3½-inch round glass or ramakin. With a sharp knife, make four equally spaced cuts from the center mark to the edge, leaving the center circle uncut.

Make another cut in the center of each of the 4 sections, and then again in each of the 8 sections, for a total of 16 sections.

Take 2 neighboring sections and twist the dough away from each other in three rotations. Pinch the end of the dough to make points of the star.

Preheat oven to 350°F. Cover star with a sheet of parchment and allow to rise in a warm place for 15 minutes. Remove top parchment and brush star with egg wash. Bake until golden brown, about 30 minutes. Sift with confectioners' sugar or drizzle with Maple Glaze. Serve warm.

PREHEAT **350**°F   BAKE TIME: 25-35 MINUTES   *SERVES* **10**

Quiche is a great way to start the day. Red and green vegetables make this a healthy and festive pie for Christmas morning.

CRUST

1¼ cups flour

½ teaspoon salt

½ cup unsalted butter

3–4 tablespoons ice water

FILLING

5 eggs

2 cups milk

½ teaspoon salt

½ teaspoon black pepper

¼ cup scallions, chopped

1 cup grape tomatoes, halved

1 cup asparagus, chopped

1½ cups shredded Gruyère

1 tablespoon flour

Preheat oven to 375°F.

In a medium bowl, mix the flour and salt. Slice the butter into small pats and toss into the flour-salt mixture. Cut the butter and flour mixture with a pastry blender until you have a fine crumb. This step can also be achieved with a food processor. Be careful not to overprocess.

Turn out the crumb mixture on a pastry board or counter. Sprinkle 3 tablespoons of the ice water over the crumb mixture. Combine with your hands, squeezing the crumbs together until a dough forms. If the dough doesn't come together, add more ice water 1 tablespoon at a time until you get the dough to form.

Roll out dough on a lightly floured surface to roughly a 12-inch round. Wrap around the rolling pin and transfer to a 9-inch pie plate. Cut off any extra crust and crimp edges. Line the crust with parchment and fill with pie weights and blind bake crust for 10 minutes. After baking, reduce oven temperature to 350°F.

To make the filling, beat eggs with a wire whisk until yolks and whites are completely incorporated. Add milk, salt, and pepper. Whisk until combined. Set aside.

In a medium bowl, mix scallions, tomatoes, asparagus, cheese, and flour. Remove the pie weights and parchment from the crust. Add vegetables mixture to the crust. Pour egg mixture over vegetables.

Bake at 350°F for 50 to 60 minutes or until the top of the quiche is golden brown on top and a cake tester inserted in the middle comes out clean. Serve immediately.

PREHEAT **375°F**
REDUCE TO **350°F**

BAKE TIME: 10 MINUTES
& 50–60 MINUTES

SERVES **8**

SPINACH AND BACON MINI SOUFFLÉS

These savory, flaky soufflés are a hit with our family, and the puff pastry makes them easy to put together. —L.K.

1 (14–17-ounce) package puff pastry

Butter for ramekins

1 pound bacon, cooked crisp and drained

1 cup fresh spinach, chopped

2 scallions, chopped

1½ cups white cheddar

1 tablespoon flour

Black pepper, to taste

9 eggs, divided

1 cup milk

Allow frozen puff pastry to thaw for about 30 minutes before starting. Preheat oven to 350°F.

Grease 8 (1-cup) ramekins with butter and set aside. Cut pastry into 8 equal pieces as close to square as possible. On a lightly floured surface, roll out each piece so it is square and large enough to overlap the side of a ramekin about 1 inch. Place in prepared ramekin and allow pastry to overlap sides. Repeat for the other 7 ramekins and set aside.

Chop cooked, drained bacon into coarse pieces and place in a medium bowl. Add spinach, scallions, cheese, flour, and pepper. Stir until combined. Spoon into pastry-lined ramekins and set on a large baking sheet.

Beat 8 eggs with a wire whisk until yolks and whites are completely incorporated. Add milk and pepper. Whisk until combined. Pour over bacon mixture, dividing evenly between the 8 ramekins. Fold overhanging pastry over the egg and bacon mixture. Beat remaining egg and brush over top pastry of each soufflé.

Bake at 350°F for 25 to 30 minutes or until the top of the soufflés are golden brown on top and a cake tester inserted in the middle comes out clean.

PREHEAT **350°F** BAKE TIME: 25-30 MINUTES *MAKES* **8**

FAST & EASY

OVERNIGHT EGG BAKE

This is a great make-ahead breakfast for a busy Christmas morning. You can prepare it the night before, refrigerate it, and bake it in the morning for an easy, delicious breakfast.

1 pound ground sausage

1 pound French bread

2½ cups shredded cheddar

9 eggs

2½ cups milk

½ teaspoon salt

½ teaspoon black pepper

1 teaspoon Worcestershire sauce

1 tablespoon butter, melted

¼ cup chives, chopped

Spray a 9-by-13-inch pan or casserole dish with nonstick spray. Brown sausage in a medium frying pan and drain off grease. Set aside.

Cut bread into 1-inch cubes. Place half the cubes in prepared pan. Cover evenly with sausage and top sausage with cheese. Cover the cheese with the other half of the bread cubes.

Beat eggs with a wire whisk until yolks and whites are completely incorporated. Add milk, salt, pepper, and Worcestershire sauce. Whisk until combined. Pour evenly over bread. Press down any bread cubes that aren't coated in egg, so that all bread is soaked in egg. Brush melted butter on the top of the bread with a pastry brush. If baking later, cover with foil and refrigerate until ready to bake.

When ready to bake, preheat oven to 350°F. Uncover pan and place in over. Bake for 45 to 50 minutes or until the top of the bread is golden and a cake tester inserted in the middle comes out clean. Top with fresh chives and serve immediately.

PREHEAT **350°F**   BAKE TIME: 45–50 MINUTES   *SERVES* **12**

VEGETABLE AND EGG SKILLET

Here's a delicious way to eat a rainbow of vegetables. This skillet of goodness is a fitting breakfast when hosting overnight guests. Serve with toast or muffins for a great start to Christmas Day.

1 tablespoon olive oil

2 teaspoons butter

3 cups shredded potatoes

1 medium red onion, peeled and chopped

2 bell peppers, cored and chopped

1 cup spinach, chopped

1 cup grape tomatoes, sliced

Salt and pepper, to taste

7 eggs

2 scallions, sliced

1 tablespoon chopped cilantro, optional

Preheat oven to 350°F.

Heat oil and butter in a 12-inch skillet over medium-high heat. Add shredded potatoes and cook for 5 minutes, scraping the bottom of the pan to keep them from sticking. Reduce to medium heat and add onion and peppers. Cook for another 4 minutes. Remove from heat and stir in spinach, tomatoes, salt, and pepper.

Make 7 wells in the vegetable mixture. Crack one egg in each well. Sprinkle a little more salt on each egg. Using hot pads, place skillet in oven. Bake 14 minutes for soft yolks or 18 minutes for hard yolks. Top with scallions and cilantro, if using, and serve immediately.

PREHEAT **350°F**   BAKE TIME: 14-18 MINUTES   *SERVES* **6**

PECAN MAPLE MUFFINS

These comforting muffins are best right out of the oven and perfect for any winter morning.

MUFFINS

½ cup butter, softened

¼ cup sugar

⅓ cup pure maple syrup, room temperature

2 eggs, room temperature

1 tablespoon vanilla extract

1 teaspoon maple extract

2 cups flour

1 teaspoon baking powder

1 teaspoon baking soda

½ teaspoon salt

½ teaspoon cinnamon

¼ cup pecans, coarsely chopped

½ cup buttermilk

TOPPING

2 tablespoons butter, melted

3 tablespoons brown sugar

¼ cup flour

¼ cup pecans, finely chopped

½ teaspoon cinnamon

Preheat oven to 350°F. Spray a 12-cup muffin pan with nonstick spray and set aside.

In a medium mixing bowl, beat butter, sugar, and maple syrup until light and fluffy, about 3 minutes. Scrape the sides and the bottom of the bowl in the middle of mixing time to ensure even mixing. Add eggs, vanilla, and maple extract and beat until combined.

In a small mixing bowl, combine flour, baking powder, baking soda, salt, cinnamon, and pecans. Add to the butter mixture and beat for one minute. Add buttermilk and beat just until combined. Scrape the sides and bottom of the bowl with a rubber spatula and stir by hand to ensure even mixing. Scoop batter into prepared pan and set aside.

To make topping, combine all ingredients in a medium bowl. With your hands, break up mixture into a crumb. Crumble over muffin batter, evenly dividing between the 12 muffins.

Bake for 18 to 20 minutes or until tops of muffins are golden brown and a cake tester inserted comes out clean. Serve muffins fresh and warm or store in an airtight container for up to 2 days. Freeze for up to 3 months.

PREHEAT **350°F**   BAKE TIME: 18-20 MINUTES   *MAKES* **12**

POPOVERS

Popovers are one of my favorite breakfast treats. Try them with lots of butter and jam. They make a great addition to a breakfast or brunch spread.

1½ tablespoons butter, plus more for the pan

1¾ cups whole milk, room temperature

1½ cups flour

½ teaspoon salt

3 eggs, room temperature

Butter a popover pan or muffin tin generously and set aside. Preheat oven to 450°F.

Melt butter and allow to cool. In a medium bowl, beat butter, milk, flour, and salt until well blended, about 2 to 3 minutes. Add eggs one at a time, beating well after each addition.

Divide batter evenly between 12 popover or muffin cups. Don't fill more than three quarters full.

Bake for 15 minutes. Reduce heat to 350°F and bake for 15 to 17 more minutes or until popovers are golden brown. Do not open the oven door while baking. Doing so may deflate the popovers. Remove from oven and poke each one with a sharp knife to allow steam to escape. Serve hot.

PREHEAT **450°F**
REDUCE TO **350°F**

BAKE TIME: 15 MINUTES
& 15-17 MINUTES

MAKES **12**

CRANBERRY PISTACHIO SCONES

Scones are a favorite in our family, and I love to create new variations. These flaky beauties are a joy on Christmas morning with coffee or tea. —L.K.

4 cups flour

½ cup cornstarch

1½ teaspoons baking soda

1 teaspoon salt

1 teaspoon cream of tartar

3 tablespoons brown sugar

1 cup unsalted butter

2¼ cups heavy cream

1 tablespoon vanilla extract

½ cup dried cranberries

⅓ cup pistachios, chopped

¼ cup unsweetened coconut flakes

Vanilla Bean Glaze (see page 234)

¼ cup pistachios, finely chopped

Preheat oven to 350°F.

In a medium bowl, mix the flour, cornstarch, baking soda, salt, cream of tartar, and brown sugar. Slice the butter into small pats and toss into the flour mixture. Cut the butter and flour mixture with a pastry blender until you have a fine crumb. This step can also be achieved with a food processor.

In a mixing bowl, combine heavy cream and vanilla. Add flour mixture. Mix in cranberries, pistachios, and coconut.

Stir together with a wooden spoon or rubber spatula.

When liquid is mostly worked into the dry ingredients, turn out onto a pastry board or countertop. Finish combining with hands just until the dough holds together.

Form a long rectangle with the dough, roughly 24 inches by 3½ inches, about ¾ inch thick.

With a sharp knife, cut the rectangle in half crosswise. Cut each half in half, and then each of these pieces in half to create 8 squares.

For large scones, cut each square diagonally to create 16 triangles. For small scones, cut an x in each square to make 32 small triangles.

Place scones on cookie sheet, leaving 1 inch between scones. Bake approximately 25 minutes for large scones, and 20 minutes for small scones. Scones will be lightly browned when ready. Repeat this step until all dough has been baked.

Place a sheet of parchment under a cooling rack. Allow scones to cool on the rack. After scones have cooled completely, spoon glaze over the top of each. Some glaze will drip off onto the parchment. Sprinkle with pistachios. Allow glaze to dry for about 45 minutes. Store scones in an airtight container for up to 3 days. Scones taste best on the day they are baked, so it's best to freeze any that you will not eat right away.

tip
If you freeze scones immediately, they will be almost as good as the day they were baked. To reheat scones, preheat oven to 290°F, place frozen scones on foil, and bake for about 12 minutes.

PREHEAT **350°F**   BAKE TIME: 20–25 MINUTES   *MAKES* **16**

BUTTERMILK CINNAMON MAPLE SCONES

These scones bring together some of the best flavors of breakfast. Try them with your favorite jam.

4 cups flour

½ cup cornstarch

1½ teaspoons baking soda

1 teaspoon salt

1 teaspoon cream of tartar

1½ teaspoons cinnamon

1 cup unsalted butter

¾ cup cinnamon chips

1 cup buttermilk

1 cup heavy cream

¼ cup pure maple syrup

½ teaspoon maple extract

Maple Glaze (see page 234)

Preheat oven to 350°F.

In a medium bowl, mix the flour, cornstarch, baking soda, salt, cream of tartar, and cinnamon. Slice the butter into small pats and toss into the flour mixture. Cut the butter and flour mixture with a pastry blender until you have a fine crumb. This step can also be achieved with a food processor. Be careful not to overprocess. Stir in cinnamon chips by hand.

In a mixing bowl, combine buttermilk, heavy cream, maple syrup, and maple extract. Pour flour over mixture. Stir together with a wooden spoon or rubber spatula. When liquid is mostly worked into the dry ingredients, turn out onto a pastry board or countertop. Finish combining with hands just until the dough holds together.

Form a long rectangle with the dough, roughly 24 inches by 3½ inches, about ¾ inch thick.

With a sharp knife, cut the rectangle in half crosswise. Cut each half in half, and then each of these pieces in half to create 8 squares. For large scones, cut each square diagonally to create 16 triangles. For small scones, cut an x in each square to make 32 small triangles.

(continued)

Place scones on cookie sheet, leaving 1 inch between scones. Bake approximately 25 minutes for large scones and 20 minutes for small scones. Scones will be a light brown when ready. Repeat this step until all dough has been baked.

Place a sheet of parchment under a cooling rack. Allow scones to cool on the rack. After scones have cooled completely, spoon glaze over the top of each. Some glaze will drip off onto the parchment. Allow glaze to dry for about 45 minutes. Store scones in an airtight container for up to 3 days. Scones taste best on the day they are baked, so it's best to freeze any that you will not eat right away.

PREHEAT **350°F**   BAKE TIME: 20–25 MINUTES   *MAKES* **16**

tip | Cinnamon chips can be found near the chocolate chips in supermarkets. Or try Cinnamon Sweet Bits from King Arthur Flour.

My high school friend Norma shared this recipe with me. These fun, sweet trees are a family tradition. Decorate yours with your favorite embellishments for a sweet Christmas morning. —J.K.

DOUGH

4½–5 cups flour

2 packages active dry yeast

1¼ cups milk

½ cup unsalted butter

¼ cup sugar

1 teaspoon salt

2 eggs

1 egg yolk (save white for filling)

FILLING

8 ounces almond paste, grated

½ cup finely chopped almonds

¼ cup unsalted butter, softened

1 egg white

1 tablespoon unsalted butter, melted

ICING

1¼ cups confectioners' sugar

2–3 tablespoons milk

½ teaspoon vanilla extract

OPTIONAL GARNISH

Sprinkles, popcorn, mini M&M's, and mini chocolate chips

To make the dough: combine 2 cups flour and yeast in mixer bowl. Combine milk, butter, sugar, and salt in saucepan and heat to very warm (about 120°F). Add milk mixture, eggs, and yolk to flour mixture and beat for 1 minute at low speed, then beat 3 minutes at high speed. Scrape bowl to get it all mixed in good.

Switch to the dough hook. Add another cup flour and beat one minute. Add enough more flour, about 1½ cups, to form soft dough. Turn onto floured surface and knead 5 to 10 minutes until smooth. Place in buttered bowl and flip once so all sides are buttered. Cover with plastic wrap and a towel. Allow to rise in warm place until doubled in size, about 1 to 1½ hours.

To make filling, mix grated almond paste, chopped almonds, butter, and egg white and set aside.

After the dough has doubled, punch down center with fist, push edges of dough into center. Turn onto floured counter, cover with a towel and let rest for 10 minutes.

Preheat oven to 350°F. Roll dough into 14-inch square. Spread filling on dough and fold two opposite sides over filling slightly overlapping. With rolling pin roll to make a 14 inch-by-9 inch rectangle. Cut 2-inch strip off 9-inch side and reserve for tree trunks.

(continued)

To form trees, cut a triangle from top center to bottom outside corners. Move triangle to a baking sheet. Place remaining smaller triangles together on a second baking sheet to form a second tree. Place long sides together. Pinch middle seam together. (See diagram.)

Cut tree trunks out of the reserved dough. Place on bottom of each tree, pinch seam. Brush trees with melted butter. Cover with towel and let raise for 40 minutes. Preheat oven to 350°F.

Bake for 15 minutes. Cool completely.

Make icing by beating together all icing ingredients for 2 minutes. Frost cooled cake with icing and decorate with optional garnish. Serve the same day or store in an airtight container for 1 day or freeze for up to 1 month.

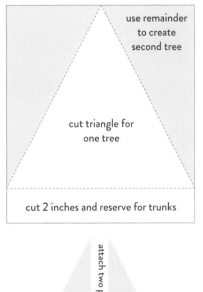

use remainder to create second tree

cut triangle for one tree

cut 2 inches and reserve for trunks

attach two pieces to form second tree

PREHEAT **350°F** · BAKE TIME: 15 MINUTES · *MAKES* **2** *TREES*

BUTTERMILK DOUGHNUTS WITH VANILLA GLAZE

Our boys love to help make (and eat) doughnuts. This decadent treat is perfect for special occasions. Sprinkle the tops of your doughnuts with fun-colored sprinkles for extra flare.

DOUGHNUTS
Vegetable oil for frying
5 tablespoons unsalted butter, softened
½ cup sugar
½ cup brown sugar
2 eggs + 1 yolk, room temperature
1 teaspoon vanilla extract
3¾ cups flour
1 teaspoon baking powder
½ teaspoon baking soda
1 teaspoon salt
¾ cup buttermilk

GLAZE
⅓ cup milk
1 teaspoon vanilla extract
3½ cups confectioners' sugar
Gel food coloring, optional

Clip a candy thermometer to the side of a large, heavy-bottomed pot or Dutch oven. Add 4 inches of vegetable oil to the pot. Preheat oil over medium-low heat while you make the doughnuts. Line a baking sheet with paper towel and top with a cooling rack. Set aside.

In a medium mixing bowl, beat butter, sugars, eggs, and vanilla until light and fluffy, about 4 minutes. Scrape the sides and the bottom of the bowl in the middle of mixing time to ensure even mixing.

In a small mixing bowl, combine flour, baking powder, baking soda, and salt. Add to the butter mixture and beat until combined. Add buttermilk and beat just until combined. Scrape the sides and bottom of the bowl with a rubber spatula and stir by hand to ensure even mixing.

Generously flour a work surface and turn out dough. With floured hands, pat the dough until it is about ⅜ inch thick. Make cutouts with a round cookie cutter, about 3 inches in diameter. Use a ½-inch round cookie cutter to cut out the center. Reserve centers for doughnut holes. Reshape dough scraps and again pat the dough until it is about ⅜ inches thick. Continue making cutouts until the dough is gone.

Increase heat on oil to medium or medium-high. Wait until oil reaches a temperature between 360°F and 370°F. Use a metal spatula or slotted spoon to gently place cutout doughnuts in oil. Add as many as will fit in a single layer without crowding the pan too much. After 2 minutes, carefully flip doughnuts. Allow each to cook an additional 2 minutes on the second side. Doughnuts are ready when both sides are golden brown. When removing, allow oil to drip into pan and then place doughnut on prepared cooling rack.

After first round of doughnuts have been cooked, check temperature of oil before proceeding with the next doughnuts. Return oil to a temperature between 360°F and 370°F and proceed with the next doughnuts. Continue until all doughnuts and doughnut holes have been fried.

While doughnuts cool, make glaze. In a medium bowl, whisk together ingredients until smooth. Spread glaze on cooled doughnuts and top with sprinkles. Serve fresh or store in an airtight container for up to 2 days.

PREHEAT OIL TO **365°F** ✦ FRY TIME: 4–5 MINUTES ✦ *MAKES* **15**

OVERNIGHT BUTTERSCOTCH BREAKFAST ROLLS

My friend Sandi has been making these rolls for Christmas morning for years. Her sons and their families also carry on the tradition. They are very easy to prepare the night before and will be ready to put in the oven when you wake up—the perfect no-fuss sweet rolls. —J.K.

22 frozen dinner rolls

1 (3.4-ounce) package butterscotch pudding (not instant)

½ cup unsalted butter

¾ cup brown sugar

¾ teaspoon cinnamon

Confectioners' sugar, for garnish, optional

Spray a 10-inch tube pan with nonstick spray.

Place frozen dinner rolls in prepared pan. Sprinkle dry pudding over rolls.

Melt butter and combine with brown sugar and cinnamon. Pour butter mixture over rolls. Spray a piece of aluminum foil with nonstick spray, cover rolls, and let stand on the counter overnight.

In the morning, preheat oven 350°F. Remove foil and bake for 30 minutes.

Leave rolls in the pan for 5 minutes and then turn over onto serving plate. Sift confectioners' sugar onto rolls if using. Serve warm.

PREHEAT **350**°F   BAKE TIME: 30 MINUTES   *MAKES* **22**

EGGNOG BREAD PUDDING

Convert day-old bread to a delicious Christmas comfort food. Serve bread pudding warm as a breakfast dish or dessert. —J.K.

1 (16-ounce) loaf French bread

4 eggs

¾ cup sugar

1 quart eggnog

⅓ cup rum

1 tablespoon vanilla extract

½ teaspoon cinnamon

½ teaspoon allspice

SAUCE

⅓ cup heavy cream

1 cup sugar

½ cup unsalted butter

Spray a 9-by-13-inch pan with nonstick spray.

To make the bread pudding: Cut bread into 1-inch cubes. Place in prepared pan. Mix remaining ingredients for the bread pudding and pour over bread. Push dry pieces of bread down into egg mixture so they get soaked.

Cover pan with foil and let soak for about 30 minutes.

Preheat oven to 350°F.

Put in oven with foil on and bake 40 minutes. Take foil off and bake 10 to 15 more minutes.

To make the sauce: Cook cream, sugar, and butter in saucepan over medium-high heat. Stir constantly until it just comes to a boil. Remove from heat.

Serve bread pudding hot in bowls or ramekins. Spoon warm sauce over individual servings. Store leftovers in the refrigerator for up 4 days.

PREHEAT **350°F**   BAKE TIME: 50–55 MINUTES   *MAKES* **36**

MALTED WAFFLES
WITH RASPBERRY COMPOTE

Waffles are a favorite at our house any day of the week and are especially perfect for Christmas served with fresh raspberry compote and vanilla bean whipped cream. —L.K.

2 cups flour

¼ cup malted milk powder

1 tablespoon baking powder

1 teaspoon baking soda

¼ teaspoon salt

2¼ cups buttermilk

¼ cup vegetable oil

3 eggs

1 teaspoon vanilla extract

Salted butter for the waffle iron

Raspberry Compote, see below

Pure maple syrup

Vanilla Bean Whipped Cream (see page 240)

Whisk together dry ingredients in a medium bowl and set aside.

In a spouted bowl, whisk together buttermilk, oil, eggs, and vanilla. Beat by hand until completely combined and a little foamy.

Pour the dry ingredients into the spouted bowl and stir with a rubber spatula, just until combined. The batter will be a little lumpy.

Preheat waffle iron. Butter iron and pour in batter until the iron is about three quarters full. Cook for 3 to 5 minutes, checking for doneness after 3 minutes. Cooking time and yield will depend on the size and temperature of your iron.

Serve immediately with warm Raspberry Compote, maple syrup, and Vanilla Bean Whipped Cream.

MAKES **12**

FRESH RASPBERRY COMPOTE

2 cups raspberry

⅓ cup pure maple syrup

Cook berries and syrup in a medium saucepan over medium-high heat until berries break down and begin to bubble, about 6 minutes. Serve warm over fresh waffles.

PISTACHIO CRANBERRY GRANOLA

Using maple syrup as a sweetener doesn't yield a strong maple flavor, but with antioxidants, minerals, and vitamins, it is an excellent alternative to cane sugar. This recipe is very easy to throw together and will make bagged granola seem boring. —L.K.

DRY INGREDIENTS
4 cups old-fashioned oats (not quick oats)

1½ cups pistachios, shelled and chopped

1 cup unsweetened coconut flakes

¼ cup flax seeds

½ cup sunflower seeds

1 cup dried cranberries

LIQUID INGREDIENTS
½ cup unsalted butter

¼ cup canola oil

⅔ cup pure maple syrup

1½ teaspoons cinnamon

1 tablespoon vanilla extract

½ teaspoon salt

Preheat oven to 290°F. Line a rimmed half-sheet baking pan with parchment or a baking mat.

In a large bowl, combine the dry ingredients except cranberries.

In a small heatproof bowl, melt butter. Whisk in canola oil, maple syrup, cinnamon, vanilla, and salt. Pour liquid ingredients over dry ingredient mixture. Toss together until dry ingredients are evenly coated.

Pour mixture evenly onto the prepared pan and bake for 1 hour. When you remove the granola from the oven, allow it to cool before removing from the pan. Once granola is cool, break it into clumps, stir in cranberries, and store in an airtight container for up to 3 weeks.

PREHEAT **290°F** ✳ BAKE TIME: 1 HOUR ✳ *MAKES* **7** CUPS

CHRISTMAS YOGURT BOWLS

With so many things to indulge in over the holidays, a healthy breakfast filled with antioxidants and probiotics can be the perfect choice. These red and green bowls are an excellent way to celebrate and will make a great start to your day.

1 cup strawberries

1 cup green grapes

3 kiwis

1 cup raspberries

¼ cup chia seeds

32 ounces vanilla yogurt

½ cup Raspberry Compote
   (see page 191)

1½ cups Pistachio Cranberry Granola
   (see page 192)

Wash and cut strawberries and grapes. Peel and slice kiwis. Wash raspberries. Arrange fruit in a serving bowl or individually in smaller bowls.

Set out individual bowls with chia seeds, yogurt, Raspberry Compote, and granola. Have your family or guests build their own yogurt bowls with their favorite toppings.

SERVES 5

CHAPTER

7

WITH THE HOUSE FULL OF PEOPLE

and so much activity over the holidays, having homemade snacks on hand adds
to the cheer. A bowl of Party Mix or Caramel Corn is nice to have on the kitchen
counter for family or part of an appetizer spread at a party. Salty and sweet and
so addictive, these will call your guests back for one more handful.

CARAMEL CORN

I've always loved caramel corn from the store, but that is no match for this homemade version. My friend told me this was the best caramel corn she has ever had. Since she's over eighty years old, I figure that covers quite a few different caramel corns. Thanks for the high praise, Joy. —J.K.

7 quarts popped popcorn (approximately ¾ cup + 2 tablespoons of unpopped corn kernels)

1 cup unsalted butter

2 cups brown sugar

½ cup corn syrup

½ teaspoon salt

2 teaspoons vanilla extract

1 teaspoon baking soda

Preheat oven to 250°F. Spray two 9-by-13-inch pans with nonstick spray. Place popcorn in two prepared pans.

In a medium pan over medium-high heat, melt butter. Whisk in brown sugar, corn syrup, and salt. Once the mixture starts to boil, stir constantly, continuing to cook for 5 additional minutes.

Remove from heat and stir in vanilla and baking soda. The additions will make the mixture foam.

Pour the mixture over the popcorn in the two pans. Stir until evenly coated.

Bake for 1 hour, stirring well every 15 minutes. Place about 2 to 3 feet of parchment on the counter.

Remove from oven and allow to cool for 5 minutes in the pan. Pour out onto parchment. Allow to cool completely. Break the caramel corn into chunks and store in airtight container for up to 2 weeks.

PREHEAT **250**°F   BAKE TIME: 1 HOUR   *MAKES* **7** QUARTS

BLACK AND WHITE
KETTLE CORN

Kettle corn is one of my favorite sweet and salty Christmas treats, and the white and dark chocolate make this version even more delicious. —J.K.

KETTLE CORN
2 tablespoons vegetable oil

2 tablespoons unsalted butter

½ cup popping corn

¼ cup sugar

½ teaspoon salt

DRIZZLE
3 ounces bittersweet chocolate, coarsely chopped

2 teaspoons shortening, divided

3 ounces white chocolate, coarsely chopped

Place 2 to 3 feet of parchment on counter.

Heat oil and butter in large pot at medium-high heat.

Add popping corn, sprinkle sugar evenly over popping corn, and place lid on pot.

When it starts to pop, shake the pot back and forth to prevent burning.

When popping slows, remove from burner and set cover ajar to let out the steam. When popping stops, uncover and sprinkle with salt. Allow to cool for 2 to 3 minutes and then pour out onto prepared parchment.

In a double boiler, heat 2 inches of water to just a simmer in bottom pan. Place bittersweet chocolate and 1 teaspoon of shortening in top pan, taking care not to spill any water into the chocolate. Stir chocolate with a rubber spatula until chocolate and shortening are completely melted and incorporated. Remove top pan and wipe water from the bottom with towel. Drizzle chocolate over kettle corn with fast motion.

Clean top double-boiler pan, careful to wipe it totally dry, and repeat drizzle process with the white chocolate. Allow chocolate to set completely. Break up pieces and store in an airtight container for up to 2 weeks.

MAKES **12** CUPS

Cookies and Cream
Party Mix

Black and White
Kettle Corn

COOKIES AND CREAM PARTY MIX

These cute little black-and-white treats will be a favorite with anyone with a sweet tooth, especially kids.

25 Oreo cookies

½ cup confectioners' sugar

6 cups Rice Chex

12 ounces white chocolate, coarsely chopped

Place 2 to 3 feet parchment onto countertop. Place cookies in a gallon-sized ziptop bag and crush with a rolling pin until you have small pieces. Add confectioners' sugar to bag and shake to mix.

Pour Chex in a large bowl and set aside.

In a medium heatproof bowl, melt chocolate in microwave in 20-second intervals. To avoid burning chocolate, stir between microwaving and remove when chocolate is mostly melted. Stir until completely melted. Pour over cereal and stir until well coated.

Pour chocolate-coated Chex into bag with cookie mixture. Shake and mix until coated with cookie mixture.

Pour onto prepared parchment and let dry. Store in airtight container for up to 2 weeks.

MAKES **12** CUPS

FESTIVE WHITE CHOCOLATE POPCORN

Fun and snackable—this popcorn is addictive. Your kids or grandkids will love to help with this simple-to-make recipe. —J.K.

3 quarts popped popcorn (approximately 6 tablespoons of unpopped corn kernels)

2 cups mini pretzels

1½ cups red and green M&M's

12 ounces white chocolate, coarsely chopped

3 tablespoons sprinkles

Place 2 to 3 feet parchment onto countertop.

Mix popcorn, pretzels, and M&M's in a large bowl.

In a medium heatproof bowl, melt chocolate in microwave in 20-second intervals. To avoid burning chocolate, stir between microwaving and remove when chocolate is mostly melted. Stir until completely melted.

Pour over popcorn mixture. Stir until it's evenly covered.

Spread onto prepared parchment. Add sprinkles immediately before chocolate gets a chance to set.

When chocolate has set, break into pieces. Store in airtight container for up to two weeks.

MAKES **13** *CUPS*

Cinnamon Party Mix

Festive White Chocolate
Popcorn

Chocolate Peanut Butter Party Mix

CHOCOLATE PEANUT BUTTER PARTY MIX

Is there anything better with peanut butter than chocolate? Put these two together in this party mix for a hit at your holiday gathering. —J.K.

6 cups Rice Chex

1 cup confectioners' sugar

1½ tablespoons cocoa

1 cup semisweet chocolate chips

½ cup (4.5 ounces) creamy peanut butter

2 cups Peanut Butter M&M's

2 cups mini peanut butter cups

2 cups peanut butter–stuffed pretzels

Place 2 to 3 feet of parchment on counter.

Put Rice Chex in a large bowl.

Pour confectioners' sugar and cocoa in a gallon-sized ziptop bag and mix.

In a medium heatproof bowl, melt chocolate and peanut butter in microwave in 20-second intervals. To avoid burning chocolate, stir between microwaving and remove when chocolate is mostly melted. Stir until completely melted..

Pour melted chocolate and peanut butter over cereal and stir until coated. Pour coated cereal in plastic bag and shake until coated with confectioners' sugar mixture. Pour out onto prepared parchment.

When cooled and completely dry, add M&M's, mini peanut butter cups, and pretzels. Store in airtight container for up to 3 weeks.

MAKES **12** CUPS

CINNAMON SUGAR PARTY MIX

This is a super-easy and sweet party snack. I love to have a variety of party mixes, both sweet and salty, for a big get-together. —J.K.

1¼ cups confectioners' sugar

½ cup brown sugar

¼ cup white sugar

1 tablespoon cinnamon + 1 teaspoon cinnamon, divided

½ cup unsalted butter

8 cups Rice Chex

1 (11-ounce) package caramel bits

Place 2 to 3 feet of parchment on counter.

In a small bowl, mix the sugars and 1 tablespoon cinnamon and set aside.

Place butter in heatproof bowl and melt in microwave.

Pour cereal in large bowl, pour melted butter over cereal, and stir until coated. Pour sugar mixture on and stir until coated. Sprinkle 1 teaspoon cinnamon on top and stir again.

Pour on prepared parchment and allow to dry for 30 minutes. Place back in bowl and stir in caramel bits.

Store in airtight container for up to 3 weeks.

MAKES **10** CUPS

CHEESY PARTY MIX

Make this unique variation on traditional party mix in your slow cooker. It will be a great addition to a party spread. —J.K.

1 cup unsalted butter, melted

1 (2-ounce) bottle of Molly McButter Cheese Sprinkles

4 cups Rice Chex

4 cups cheese crackers

4 cups Club Minis crackers

4 cups Ritz Bits cheese crackers

2 cups mini pretzels

Place 2 to 3 feet of parchment on counter.

Melt butter and add the cheese sprinkles. Set aside.

Mix the rest of the ingredients in a 6-quart or larger slow cooker. Mix well and pour half of the butter-cheese sprinkle mixture over the cracker mixture in the slow cooker. Stir gently and then pour rest of the butter mixture over the cracker mixture. Stir, coating everything.

Cook uncovered on low for 2 hours, stirring gently every 15 minutes.

When done, pour on prepared parchment to cool. When cool, store in airtight container for up to 3 weeks.

SLOW COOKER **LOW** ✳ COOK TIME: 2 HOURS ✳ *MAKES* **18** CUPS

GOOEY COCONUT PARTY MIX

Sweet and so delicious—this sticky treat is hard to stop eating. —J.K.

4 cups **Rice Chex cereal**

4 cups **Corn Chex cereal**

4 cups **Golden Grahams cereal**

1 cup **chopped pecans**

2 cups **sweetened shredded coconut**

1 cup **sugar**

1 cup **light corn syrup**

¾ cup **salted unsalted butter**

1½ teaspoons **vanilla extract**

Place 2 to 3 feet of parchment on counter.

In large bowl, mix cereals, nuts, and coconut and set aside.

Place sugar, corn syrup, and butter in saucepan and bring to a boil. Boil for 3 minutes, stirring constantly.

Remove from heat and stir in vanilla.

Pour over cereal mixture, and stir until well coated.

Pour on prepared parchment to cool. When cool, store in airtight container for up to 2 weeks.

MAKES **13** CUPS

CARAMEL PARTY MIX

When I worked in New York, my friend Laura received an amazing Christmas care package from her mother in Minnesota. This Party Mix was part of the package and was so addictive, I had to have the recipe. Laura's mother, Ginny, was nice enough to share this, and now it's a favorite on my holiday baking list. —L.K.

10 cups Rice Chex or Corn Chex

16 ounces dry roasted peanuts

9 ounces stick pretzels

1 cup unsalted butter

2 cups brown sugar

½ cup light corn syrup

Preheat oven to 350°F.

In a large bowl, combine Chex, peanuts, and pretzels. Prepare two 9-by-13-inch pans with nonstick spray and set aside.

In a medium pan over medium-high heat, melt butter. Whisk in brown sugar and corn syrup. Once the mixture starts to boil, stir constantly for 2 minutes. Pour hot mixture over Chex mixture. Stir until evenly coated. Transfer to prepared pans and place in oven. Bake for 16 minutes. Stir once in the middle of the baking time.

Remove from oven and allow to cool for about 5 minutes in the pan. Place 2 to 3 feet of parchment on counter. Pour Party Mix on parchment. Allow to cool completely. Break the caramel Chex into chunks and store in airtight container for up to 3 weeks.

PREHEAT **350°F**   BAKE TIME: 16 MINUTES   *MAKES* **12** CUPS

HAVE A VERY HYGGE CHRISTMAS

with these cozy drinks. Grab a hot mug of peppermint mocha, a warm throw, and a book and snuggle up by the fire on a wintry night. The kids will love the rich hot chocolate after playing in the snow. Hot and cold, sweet with a little bit of spice—these drinks will bring comfort and joy to your season.

HOT CHOCOLATE

If a brownie could be a hot beverage, this is what it would taste like. Using real chocolate instead of the powdered hot chocolate envelopes makes a much more decadent drink.

4 cups whole milk

¼ superfine sugar

6 ounces bittersweet chocolate, coarsely chopped

2 teaspoons vanilla extract

4 Vanilla Bean Marshmallows (see page 133)

In a medium pot over medium-high heat, cook milk and sugar. Whisk until sugar has completely dissolved. Add chocolate and whisk until melted and incorporated. Add vanilla and continue heating until steaming hot but not boiling.

Pour into 4 mugs and top each with a homemade marshmallow.

COOK TIME: 5-10 MINUTES

SERVES **4**

tip || You can use regular sugar instead of superfine sugar; it will just take a little longer for it to dissolve.

PEPPERMINT MOCHA

Winter is the time to seek out cozy comforts. When there's a chill in the air, snuggle in with a hot mug of peppermint mocha for a little sweet contentment.

3 cups strong coffee

2 cups milk

3 ounces bittersweet chocolate, coarsely chopped

⅓ cup crème de menthe

¾ cup whipped cream, optional

Peppermint stick, optional

Brew strong coffee with a French press or a traditional drip coffee maker by adding extra coffee grounds. You can also use a finer-ground coffee to achieve stronger flavor.

In a medium pot over medium heat, cook milk. Add chocolate and whisk until it is completely melted and incorporated with the milk. Add the crème de menthe and coffee. Whisk together and cook until steaming hot but not boiling.

Pour into 4 mugs. Top with whipped cream and serve with peppermint stick, if using.

COOK TIME: 5–10 MINUTES

SERVES 4

The word *wassail* derives from an Anglo Saxon greeting meaning "be healthful" that was part of a medieval Christmastime tradition of wassailing—singing, house-visiting, and drinking spiced cider and ale. As the carol goes, "Love and joy come to you / And to you a Wassail too / God bless you and send you, / A happy new year." This version of hot mulled cider is perfect to share at a party to wish your guests cheer and good health.

½ gallon apple cider

2 cups orange juice

1 teaspoon ground cloves

1 teaspoon allspice

1 teaspoon ground cinnamon

4 cinnamon sticks

2 star anise

1 orange, sliced

1 apple, sliced

In a medium pot over medium-high heat, cook cider and juice. Add ground cloves, allspice, and ground cinnamon; whisk until dissolved. Add cinnamon sticks, star anise, and orange and apple slices. Bring mixture to a boil. Reduce temperature to medium-low and allow to simmer for 45 minutes.

Before serving, remove cinnamon sticks and star anise with a slotted spoon. Fill mugs using a soup ladle or transfer hot cider to a crockpot to keep hot and allow guests to serve themselves.

COOK TIME: 45–50 MINUTES

SERVES **8**

MOCHA MILKSHAKE PUNCH

Based on my daughter-in-law's family's traditional Christmas punch, this is a merry addition to a holiday celebration. Just don't let the little ones have too much. One year, my grandson had a generous serving and ended up bouncing off the walls way past his bedtime. —J.K.

8 cups strong coffee

⅔ cup sugar

6 ounces bittersweet chocolate, coarsely chopped

½ gallon vanilla ice cream

½ gallon chocolate ice cream

GARNISH

2 cups whipped cream

Mini chocolate chips

Chocolate sprinkles

Crushed peppermint candies

Crème de menthe syrup, optional

Heat freshly brewed coffee over medium heat in a large saucepan. Add sugar and chocolate and whisk until chocolate has completely melted and incorporated into coffee. Allow to cool. Pour into a pitcher, cover, and refrigerate for 2 hours or overnight.

About 10 minutes before serving, pour cold coffee mixture into a large punch bowl and stir. With an ice cream scoop, create balls out of both half gallons ice cream and add to punch bowl. Stir until partially melted. Serve with optional garnishes and allow guests to customize their mocha milkshakes.

For mint mocha, guests can add a shot of crème de menthe syrup and top with whipped cream and crushed peppermint candies.

COOK TIME: 5-10 MINUTES

SERVES **15**

CHRISTMAS SANGRIA

If you're looking for a fruity libation for a holiday party, try this festive sangria. For a nonalcoholic version, replace the wine with nonalcoholic white wine and omit rum.

2 small Granny Smith apples

1 pomegranate

1 bottle white wine

Juice of 1 lime

¼ cup Simple Syrup (see page 248)

¼ cup rum

GARNISH

Lime wedge

Demerara sugar (or other coarse sugar)

Wash and core apples. Cut into small cubes. Place in a large pitcher. Remove seeds from pomegranate and combine with apple. Pour wine over fruit. Add lime juice, simple syrup, and rum. Stir well. Cover pitcher with plastic wrap and refrigerate for 1 to 2 hours and serve on the same day.

To serve, run a lime wedge around the rim of each serving glass. Dip the rim of glass in demerara sugar. Fill glass halfway with ice, spoon some fruit from the pitcher over ice, and pour sangria over ice and fruit.

COOL TIME: 1-2 HOURS

SERVES **6**

CHAPTER

9

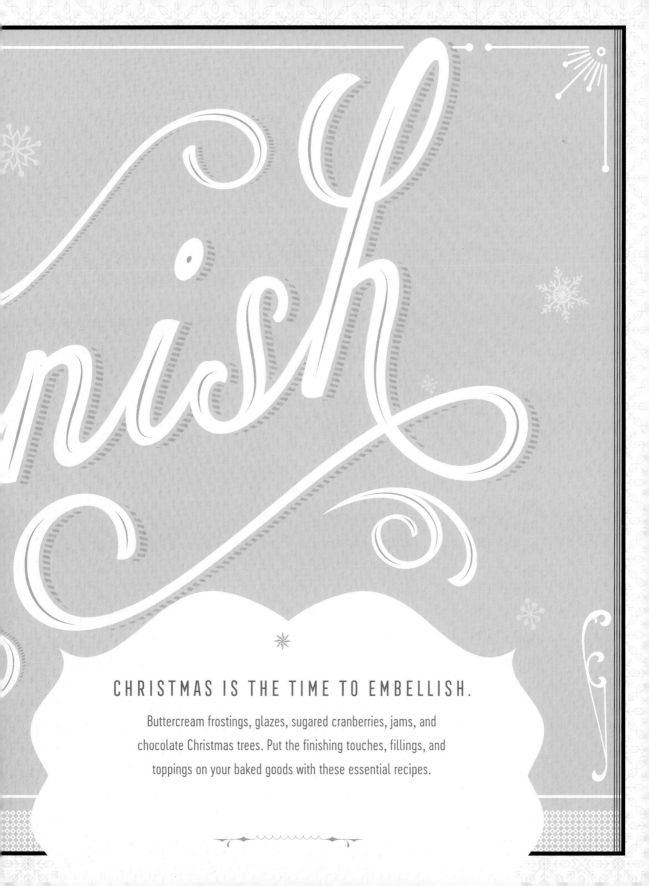

CHRISTMAS IS THE TIME TO EMBELLISH.

Buttercream frostings, glazes, sugared cranberries, jams, and
chocolate Christmas trees. Put the finishing touches, fillings, and
toppings on your baked goods with these essential recipes.

SUGARED CRANBERRIES

I love having these beauties on hand over the holidays to garnish cakes or add to a table of treats and snacks. Cranberries are typically in season in November and December, so take advantage of fresh berries. —L.K.

2¼ cups sugar, divided
1 teaspoon almond extract
1 cup water
2 cups fresh cranberries

In a medium saucepan over medium-high heat, boil 1 cup sugar, almond extract, and water to make simple syrup. Boil until the sugar is completely dissolved. Allow to cool for 10 minutes and then add cranberries. Allow to cool completely.

Place a cooling rack on a cookie sheet. When simple syrup is completely cool, remove cranberries with a slotted spoon. Place them on the cooling rack to allow them to dry. Separate each cranberry so none are touching each other. Allow cranberries to dry for about 1 hour. You will know they are ready when they stick to your finger.

Pour the remiaing sugar into a medium bowl. Coat cranberries in the sugar, taking care they don't stick to each other. Place them in a bowl to serve or in a single layer in an airtight container to store. Sugared cranberries will keep in the refrigerator for up to 1 week.

MAKES **2** *CUPS*

RASPBERRY JAM

It's great to have homemade jam on hand for popovers, Linzer cookies, Kolaczki, or even your morning toast.

3 cups raspberries

1¼ cups sugar

2 tablespoons lemon juice

1 tablespoon cornstarch

1 teaspoon vanilla extract

Cook raspberries, sugar, lemon juice, and cornstarch in a medium saucepan over medium-high heat. As you stir, raspberries will break down and turn to liquid. Bring mixture to a boil. Reduce temperature to medium. Cook and stir until the mixture coats the back of the spoon, about 8 to 9 minutes. Keep in mind jam will thicken more when it has cooled. Stir in vanilla.

Pour into a glass pint jar and store in the refrigerator for up to 4 weeks.

COOK TIME: 10–13 MINUTES

MAKES **1½** CUPS

CRANBERRY ALMOND JAM

Cranberry jam is perfect for Christmas morning scones or used in thumbprint cookies.

3 cups cranberries
⅓ cup orange juice
1½ cups sugar
1 tablespoon cornstarch
1 teaspoon almond extract

Process cranberries and orange juice in food processor or blender until all berries are broken down. Add cranberry and orange juice mixture to a medium saucepan and cook over medium-high heat. Add sugar and cornstarch and bring mixture to a boil. Reduce temperature to medium. Cook and stir until the mixture coats the back of the spoon, about 8 to 9 minutes. Keep in mind jam will thicken more when it has cooled. Stir in almond extract.

Pour into a glass pint jar and store in the refrigerator for up to 4 weeks.

COOK TIME: 10–13 MINUTES

MAKES **1½** CUPS

GARNISH

DULCE DE LECHE

Common in Latin America, dulce de leche is a little different from caramel, though it has a similar flavor. It goes great in sandwich cookies or as a dip for apples or poured on ice cream.

4 cups whole milk

1½ cups sugar

½ teaspoon baking soda

1 tablespoon vanilla bean paste

In a large heavy-bottomed pot or Dutch oven, combine milk and sugar. Cook over medium-high heat, whisking until sugar is completely dissolved. Add baking soda and vanilla bean paste. Cook until boiling. The mixture will foam up high at this stage. Stir constantly and reduce heat if foam gets to the top of pot. After mixture boils, reduce temperature to low and simmer, stirring occasionally. Cook until thick and golden brown, between 1 and 2 hours.

Pour into a glass pint jar and store in the refrigerator for up to 4 weeks.

COOK TIME: 1–2 HOURS

MAKES **1** CUP

note Stoves produce different levels of heat, so cook time will vary depending on your stove.

MAPLE GLAZE

⅓ cup pure maple syrup

1¼ cups confectioners' sugar

¼ teaspoon maple extract, optional

½ teaspoon vanilla extract

Whisk together ingredients until smooth and fluid. At first, it may seem there is too much confectioners' sugar, but the mixture will come together. If it's too thick, add milk or more maple syrup, ½ teaspoon at a time.

MAKES 3/4 CUPS

VANILLA BEAN GLAZE

¼ cup half-and-half

1 teaspoon vanilla bean paste

1½ cups confectioners' sugar

Whisk together ingredients until smooth and fluid. At first, it may seem that there is too much confectioners' sugar, but the mixture will come together. If it's too thick, add half-and-half, ½ teaspoon at a time.

MAKES 3/4 CUPS

VANILLA BUTTERCREAM

This is my go-to buttercream base for cookies and cakes. It's similar to the dense buttercream frostings that you find in New York City cupcake bakeries. Keep in mind that, when cold, the butter in this recipe will make the buttercream quite hard. So if you do refrigerate this frosting, be sure to set it out 1 hour in advance of serving it. —L.K.

1 cup unsalted butter, room temperature

⅓ cup heavy cream, room temperature

1 tablespoon vanilla extract or vanilla bean paste

5–5½ cups confectioners' sugar

Using a stand mixer with the paddle attachment, beat the butter, heavy cream, vanilla, and 1 cup of the confectioners' sugar for 3 minutes until fluffy. Scrape the bowl, including the bottom, to make sure all ingredients are being incorporated.

Add remaining confectioners' sugar ½ cup at a time, beating well in between each addition until you reach a spreadable consistency. You can always add a little more cream if your frosting is too thick or a little more confectioners' sugar if it's too thin.

tip   Temperature matters when working toward the right consistency with buttercream frostings. Working with all ingredients at room temperature will make it easier to judge the right consistency for your cake or cookie.

MAKES ABOUT 4¾ CUPS

half batch   Use a half batch when making cookies or fillings. Here's a handy breakdown of ingredients in a half batch.

½ cup unsalted butter, room temperature
3 tablespoons heavy cream, room temperature
1½ teaspoons vanilla extract or vanilla bean paste
2½–2¾ cups confectioners' sugar
Food coloring, optional

RASPBERRY BUTTERCREAM

I love this combination of buttercream and raspberry. I also love its pink appearance speckled with red bits of raspberry—a perfect look for Christmas. —L.K.

1 cup unsalted butter, room temperature

¼ cup pure maple syrup, room temperature

⅓ cup heavy cream, room temperature

1 tablespoon vanilla extract

⅓ cup Raspberry Jam, room temperature (see page 230)

6–7 cups confectioners' sugar

Using a stand mixer with the paddle attachment, beat the butter, maple syrup, heavy cream, vanilla, raspberry jam, and 1 cup of the confectioners' sugar for 3 minutes until fluffy. Scrape the bowl, including the bottom, to make sure all ingredients are being incorporated.

Add remaining confectioners' sugar ½ cup at a time, beating well in between each addition until you reach a spreadable consistency. You can always add a little more cream if your frosting is too thick or a little more confectioners' sugar if it's too thin.

MAKES ABOUT **5** *CUPS*

half batch

Use a half batch when making cookies or fillings.
Here's a handy breakdown of ingredients in a half batch.

½ cup unsalted butter, room temperature
2 tablespoons pure maple syrup
3 tablespoons heavy cream, room temperature
3 tablespoons raspberry jam, room temperature (see page 230)
1½ teaspoons vanilla extract or vanilla bean paste
3–3½ cups confectioners' sugar

CHOCOLATE BUTTERCREAM

Add a layer of rich chocolate to cakes and cookies with this intensely fudgy buttercream.

6 ounces bittersweet chocolate

1 cup unsalted butter, room temperature

¼ cup heavy cream, room temperature

1 tablespoon vanilla extract

3–3½ cups confectioners' sugar

¾ cup unsweetened cocoa

Melt chocolate and allow to cool.

Using a stand mixer with the paddle attachment, beat the butter, chocolate, heavy cream, vanilla, and 1 cup of the confectioners' sugar for 3 minutes until fluffy. Scrape the bowl, including the bottom, to make sure all ingredients are being incorporated.

Sift cocoa into bowl and beat until incorporated.

Add remaining confectioners' sugar ½ cup at a time, beating well in between each addition until you reach a spreadable consistency. You can always add a little more cream if your frosting is too thick or a little more confectioners' sugar if it's too thin.

tip This buttercream will become quite stiff if refrigerated. If refrigerating, remove from refrigerator one hour before serving.

MAKES ABOUT 4½ CUPS

half batch

Use a half batch when making cookies or fillings. Here's a handy breakdown of ingredients in a half batch.

½ cup unsalted butter, room temperature
3 ounces bittersweet chocolate
2 tablespoons heavy cream, room temperature
1½ teaspoons vanilla extract
6 tablespoons unsweetened cocoa
1½–1¾ cups confectioners' sugar

CREAM CHEESE FROSTING

Cream cheese frosting is amazing on Soft Vanilla Cookies (see page 26). It's also essential to Red Velvet Cake (see page 137).

16 ounces cream cheese, room temperature

½ cup unsalted butter, room temperature

2 teaspoons vanilla extract

5–5½ cups confectioners' sugar

Using a stand mixer with the paddle attachment, beat the cream cheese, butter, vanilla, and 1 cup of the confectioners' sugar for 3 minutes until fluffy. Scrape the bowl, including the bottom, to make sure all ingredients are being incorporated.

Add confectioners' sugar ½ cup at a time, beating well in between each addition until you reach a spreadable consistency.

MAKES ABOUT **4** *CUPS*

VANILLA BEAN WHIPPED CREAM

Real whipped cream is the perfect complement to fruit-based desserts. Try this version with vanilla bean paste for extra flavor.

2 cups heavy cream

1 teaspoon vanilla bean paste

3 tablespoons confectioners' sugar

Combine ingredients in a medium mixing bowl or the bowl of a stand mixer. Beat on high with the whisk attachment until stiff peaks form. Serve immediately.

MAKES **3** *CUPS*

GARNISH

ROYAL ICING

Royal icing is essential for decorated sugar cookies. It hardens so designs will stay intact. Most royal icing recipes get very hard and have a dull finish. I created this version so the icing hardens on the outside, but is still a little soft inside and has a little shine. —L.K.

½ cup water

3 tablespoons meringue powder

2 tablespoons heavy cream

1 tablespoon corn syrup

1 teaspoon vanilla extract

5½ to 6½ cups confectioners' sugar

Gel food coloring, optional

Using a stand mixer with the whisk attachment, beat water, meringue powder, heavy cream, corn syrup, and vanilla for 2 minutes until well combined.

Add confectioners' sugar 1 cup at a time, beating well in between each addition. After 5 cups add confectioners' sugar ½ cup at a time until you reach your desired consistency. You can always add a little more water if your icing is too thick or a little more confectioners' sugar if it's too thin.

Scrape the bowl, including the bottom, to make sure all ingredients are being incorporated and beat for two more minutes.

Divide icing into bowls and color with gel food coloring if desired.

MAKES 4 CUPS

Attach a tip to a piping bag. Fold the top of piping bag over a glass.

Pour icing into opening at top of glass.

Tie top of piping bag with baker's twine. Royal icing is very thin and will easily run out the top of the bag, so tie top as tightly as possible.

Repeat process for all colors.

WHITE CHOCOLATE CHRISTMAS TREES

These cute cake toppers are perfect for a holiday party and are fun to make with kids. —L.K.

12 Pocky sticks or lollipop sticks

Sprinkles

12 ounces white chocolate, coarsely chopped

Gel food coloring

Line counter with 3 to 4 feet of parchment. Set Pocky sticks and sprinkles next to work area.

Prepare 3 disposable piping bags with number 3 or 4 round tips. Place each piping bag in a tall glass tip down and fold the wide end of piping bag over the edge of the glass. Divide the chocolate evenly into 3 medium heatproof bowls. Melt first batch of chocolate in microwave set to 50 percent power and start with 30 seconds. Check chocolate and stir. Continue microwaving in 15-second intervals until almost completely melted. Continue to stir until completely melted. Add gel food coloring a little at a time and stir completely. Pour into one of the prepared piping bags.

Pipe a dot of chocolate on prepared parchment and set one stick in chocolate to hold it in place.

Form a triangle by piping chocolate back and forth across stick, starting at the top point and getting wider as you go down. Leave 1 to 2 inches of stick bare at bottom. Decorate tree with sprinkles before chocolate sets.

(continued)

Continue making trees until chocolate is gone. Vary height and width of trees. Repeat process with remaining bowls of chocolate, creating a different color for each.

Allow chocolate to set completely. Store in an airtight container until ready to use. Poke sticks into top of cake when ready to display. If bringing cake to a party, wait to add trees to cake until after transporting.

GINGERBREAD SPICE

If you love gingerbread, and are planning to do a lot of baking, you can premix your gingerbread spices to simplify baking. Recipes in this book have measurements listed individually or using this combination of spices.

3 tablespoons ground ginger
3 tablespoons cinnamon
1 tablespoon allspice
1 tablespoon ground cloves

Combine spices in a small bowl with a whisk. Store in a mini canister or spice jar. To use in a gingerbread recipe, replace total amounts of spice with gingerbread spice.

MAKES **¹/₂** *CUP*

SIMPLE SYRUP

Like its name implies, this is easy to make and handy for mixing in drinks or brushing on cake layers for extra-moist cake.

1 cup sugar

1 cup water

In a small saucepan, combine sugar and water and cook over medium-high heat. Bring to a boil for 1 minute. Remove from heat and allow to cool completely. Pour into a jar, seal, and store in the refrigerator for up to 3 weeks.

MAKES **1¹/₃** *CUPS*

RESOURCES

CHOCOLATE

Valrhona Chocolates
www.valrhona-chocolate.com

Guittard Chocolate Company
www.guittard.com

Ghirardelli Chocolate Company
www.ghirardelli.com

Scharffen Berger Chocolate Maker
www.scharffenberger.com

EXTRACTS

Nielsen Massey Fine Vanillas and Flavors
nielsenmassey.com

Cook's
www.cooksvanilla.com

Vanilla Bean Kings
www.vanillabeankings.com

FLOURS AND SPECIALTY INGREDIENTS

King Arthur Flour
shop.kingarthurflour.com

MAPLE SYRUP

Crown Maple
www.crownmaple.com

PASTURE-RAISED EGGS

Vital Farms
vitalfarms.com

ICING TOOLS

Sweet Sugarbelle
amazon.com

Wilton
wilton.com

Ateco Baking Products
www.atecousa.com

LINZER COOKIE CUTTER SET

JOKUMO
amazon.com

COOKIE STAMPS AND BAKING PANS

Nordic Ware
www.nordicware.com

Williams Sonoma
www.williamsonoma.com

FOOD-GRADE GIFT PACKAGING

Bags and Bows
www.bagsandbows.com

ACKNOWLEDGMENTS

To all my fellow cooks and readers, you guys are the best! I so appreciate your love and encouragement.

To the people at Kean's Store Company in Mason, Michigan, for recommending *Mom's Comfort Food* to your customers and for hosting a cookbook and tasting event. I am so grateful for local stores like yours.

To the many people who shared recipes over the years, I've enjoyed your ideas and fellowship.

To Mary Knoper, my "old" friend who shared her recipe for Maple Peanut Clusters. I had so much fun figuring out the perfect version with you, sending a lot of text messages, mailing our finished products, and deciding they were yummy. Thanks for mailing me chocolate from your local Amish store in Indiana. Thanks, my friend, that was a good time.

To the many taste testers, for sharing your honest feedback.

To Alv and Joy, for the beautiful holly.

To my cousin Leah, for your friendship and helping with proofreading.

Christmas is such a special time of year—celebrating the birth of Jesus with family and friends. I hope you find some new recipes in this book that bring you comfort and joy and become gift-giving go-to's. Merry Christmas!

—*Joyce*

To my husband Gregorio, for his painting and carpentry skills. Thank you for the many hours creating studio space, building backgrounds, shopping for reclaimed wood, holding reflectors, rigging camera equipment, enduring overflowing prop closets, and supporting me even when my ideas seem crazy—which they often do.

To Victor, the best sous-chef a *tia* could ask for.

To Leo, for being the most likely person in the house to suggest baking cookies.

To Nicole Frail, our editor extraordinaire, for all your ideas and support.

To the team at Skyhorse Publishing: publisher Abigail Gehring, production editor Chris Schultz, and creative director Brian Peterson. Thank you for all the behind-the-scenes work. Publishing people are the best!

To Allison, for the greatest holiday-baking marathons ever!

To my mom, for introducing me to baking and giving.

To Betsy, for being the sister I never had.

To Amy, for the many tips on the art of making banket. Thank you for your collaborative creative spirit and friendship over the decades.

To the many art directors and colleagues who have inspired, encouraged, and shared their passion for design with me: Georgia, Michelle, Roberto, Will, Raina, Ervin, Jimmy, Richard, Mary, Phil, Laura, and Anton. I learned so much from all of you.

To Mumtaz, my best friend in creativity, and all things food, design, and photography. Your brilliance, style, laughter, and grace make the world a better place.

—Laura

CONVERSION CHARTS

METRIC AND IMPERIAL CONVERSIONS

(These conversions are rounded for convenience)

Ingredient	Cups/Tablespoons/Teaspoons	Ounces	Grams/Milliliters
Butter	1 cup/16 tablespoons/2 sticks	8 ounces	230 grams
Cheese, shredded	1 cup	4 ounces	110 grams
Cornstarch	1 tablespoon	0.3 ounce	8 grams
Cream cheese	1 tablespoon	0.5 ounce	14.5 grams
Flour, all-purpose	1 cup/1 tablespoon	4.5 ounces/0.3 ounce	125 grams/8 grams
Flour, whole wheat	1 cup	4 ounces	120 grams
Fruit, dried	1 cup	4 ounces	120 grams
Fruits or veggies, chopped	1 cup	5 to 7 ounces	145 to 200 grams
Fruits or veggies, puréed	1 cup	8.5 ounces	245 grams
Honey, maple syrup, or corn syrup	1 tablespoon	0.75 ounce	20 grams
Liquids: cream, milk, water, or juice	1 cup	8 fluid ounces	240 milliliters
Oats	1 cup	5.5 ounces	150 grams
Salt	1 teaspoon	0.2 ounces	6 grams
Spices: cinnamon, cloves, ginger, or nutmeg (ground)	1 teaspoon	0.2 ounce	5 milliliters
Sugar, brown, firmly packed	1 cup	7 ounces	200 grams
Sugar, white	1 cup/1 tablespoon	7 ounces/0.5 ounce	200 grams/12.5 grams
Vanilla extract	1 teaspoon	0.2 ounce	4 grams

OVEN TEMPERATURES

Fahrenheit	Celsius	Gas Mark
225°	110°	¼
250°	120°	½
275°	140°	1
300°	150°	2
325°	160°	3
350°	180°	4
375°	190°	5
400°	200°	6
425°	220°	7
450°	230°	8

ABOUT THE AUTHORS

JOYCE KLYNSTRA is the author of *Mom's Comfort Food: Meals, Sides, and Desserts to Bring Warmth and Contentment to Your Table*. She has loved cooking since her teenage years, which she spent working in a family-run drive-in restaurant. She continued her passion for cooking with a wedding cake business, hosting church dinners, and working in hospitality with her Army husband. She lives in Michigan.

Facebook: @joyklyn

LAURA KLYNSTRA is a freelance graphic designer and photographer focusing on book covers and illustrated book interiors. Before running her business, she worked as art director at Hyperion Books and at HarperCollins Publishers. She lives in Michigan with her husband, two boys, a dog, and a menagerie of cats, chickens, and ducks.

www.lauraklynstra.net

Instagram & Facebook: @spiceandsugartable